Sylvester Sherman

History of the 133d regiment

Sylvester Sherman

History of the 133d regiment

ISBN/EAN: 9783337115968

Printed in Europe, USA, Canada, Australia, Japan

Cover: Foto ©ninafisch / pixelio.de

More available books at **www.hansebooks.com**

History of

THE 133D REGIMENT, O. V. I.

And incidents connected with its service
during the

"WAR OF THE REBELLION."

By the Historian of the Association
of its survivors

S. M. SHERMAN, M. D.

PREFACE

To my Comrades of the 133d *Regt., O. V. I.:*

In presenting this little history of our share in the "War for the Union," I am aware how imperfect it is, but you will remember that nearly thirty-two years have passed since our service was rendered, and that this fact and that of our comrades being so widely scattered, has made it difficult to gather data.

Many items of interest could have been contributed by the comrades had it been urged upon them by personal interview, but business cares have left me scant time for this labor of love.

The memory of our Colonel has been a never failing source of information.

I also beg leave to acknowledge aid from Comrades C. N. Bancroft, John C. Ender, Rev. H. B. Westervelt, Lucius Smith, R. E. Sheldon, F. B. Dean, J. A. Oldham, Rev. H. L. Whitehead, S. W. Williams, C. H. Parsons, and others.

The official records of the war, issued by the government and other authorities, have been consulted. The roster of the regiment is from the "Official Roster of Ohio Soldiers in the War of the Rebellion," published by the State.

Yours fraternally,

S. M. SHERMAN,
Historian.

Columbus, O., April 6, 1896.

CONTENTS.

CHAPTER I.
Introduction—How we came to be in it.

CHAPTER II.
Gathering of the boys—Soldier fare—Useful hints—Camp Chase—New beds.

CHAPTER III.
How the regiment was made up—Good material—We don the blue—The regiment armed—Good bye—Families and crops to be cared for—How equipped.

CHAPTER IV.
No yankees need apply—He was afraid of war—His ardor dampened—Good news—We move on—The boys were ready to meet the rebs—New Creek—An alarm—Hard work—We ave money for Uncle Sam—Steady drill.

CHAPTER V.
Supplying outposts—Above the clouds—Picket duty—Saucy rebels—High priced pork—Religious services—Our friends alarmed—Another scare—Copperheads—At fearful cost—To the rescue—A joke that nearly proved serious—Measles and mumps get us.

CHAPTER VI.
As good as any—After guerrillas—They were ours because we needed them—Cash all gone—Some veteran officers.

CHAPTER VII.
On to Washington—Rebel work—Fine scenery—We were not much scared—Ohio was there—What we may get, maybe!—Now for real war—Tribute to the sea—Sealed orders.

Chapter VIII.

We are at the front—Stationed on the line—We build bombproofs—A strong line—In the trenches.

Chapter IX.

We fight for the Union—Tearing up the railroad—Look! They're going to charge—We give them our best—A great blunder—Our division to hold the line—Just how it was—Prisoners taken—A close call—Part ran, but came back again—The colonel stayed.

Chapter X.

We go to another post—General Butler compliments us—An army on the move—An agreeable change—Butler's idea of the place—To fight desperately—All kinds of soldiers—A troublesome task—Hostages taken—Despair of hostages—Hostages paroled—Killed by bushwhackers.

Chapter XI.

Exciting and dangerous service—Halt—Pitiful case—A run for life—Shameful outrage.

Chapter XII.

A thrilling experience—A night trip—A critical moment Our escape—Map of the locality—Ticklish reconnoitering——Rather do something else—Terrible punishment.

Chapter XIII.

Great responsibility—Be vigilant—Did not want to go--Hurry up the fortifications—Strength of garrison—Inefficient officer—A better one—Life at the fort—The neat 133d—Soul inspiring whisky—Good markmanship.

Chapter XIV.

Supply train attacked—General Sheridan hungry—In a critical situation—Wilson's raid—Peculiar wounds—Plantation darkies—Marriage not a failure—Change of diet—Superfluous—Foraging—The glorious Fourth—Fighting whisky—*Undress* uniform.

CHAPTER XV.

Drowned—A sad romance—Our deadliest enemy—Gloomy thoughts—On the alert—They're slow, but look out when they get there—Another compliment.

CHAPTER XVI.

Welcome visitors—Signal tower—We go after the rebs—Butler scolds—Bushwhackers—We leave Fort Powhatan—Taming a rebel.

CHAPTER XVII.

Back to Washington---The President wants to see us---Every one kind to soldiers---Go home---A good supper—A great welcome—Some sad hearts---We were too full—Our Grand Parade---Out.--Goodbye! Boys.

ROSTER---ROLL OF HONOR.

CHAPTER I.

INTRODUCTION

By Comrade C. N. Bancroft, Q. M. — "How we came to be in it."

When armed treason raised its hand against the unity and integrity of the Republic our Commonwealth had no organized militia such as now redounds to the credit and honor of the Buckeye State, such as our own present efficient and wellknown Ohio National Guard.

At that period the few independent companies in existence were confined to our large cities, among which were the wellknown Cleveland Grays, Guthrie Grays, Rover Guards, Columbus Videttes and the State Fencibles.

These were drilled and under good discipline and all responded to the first call of Abraham Lincoln for seventy-five thousand men.

Popular prejudice existed against militia duty up to the commencement of the "War of the Rebellion" and legislative action for fostering and organizing the militia of the State previous to the commencement of hostilities was of slow growth—showing that comparatively little had been accomplished to this end.

It is, however, an indisputable fact, that the militia of our State such as it was in 1861, was far superior to that existing in any of the Western States.

Governor Tod upon assuming his office, appreciating the general feeling as well as the palpable necessity of a more thorough organization of the State Militia in his message to the legislature at its opening session in January 1863, called attention to these facts, and that body wrestled over a bill until the last of the session when it passed both branches, viz:

"To organize and discipline the militia of Ohio."

The act was formulated to designate the militia as "Ohio Militia" and "Ohio Volunteer Militia."

The close of the year's labors of the Adjutant General in carrying out the provisions of the bill was gratifying and resulted in enrolling in the first class 167,572 men, and in the Ohio Volunteer Militia 43,930 for five years.

During 1863 the Volunteer Militia were kept at drilling during the time prescribed by law and thus given shape and cohesion.

In February 1864, Governor Brough, comprehending the situation and believing the critical point of the war at hand, on the opening of the spring campaign, conceived the idea of calling on the Ohio National Guard and discussed with ex-Governor Dennison the importance of the movement.

At his request Governor Dennison visited Washington to confer with the Secretary of War.

Correspondence followed with the governors of other states which resulted at the suggestion of Governor Brough in a meeting at Washington of the governors of Ohio, Indiana, Illinois, Wisconsin and Iowa, to consider the question of tendering the Government the services of the State Militia from these states.

The result of this conference was that the President was tendered upon April 21, 1864, the services of 85,000 men for the period of 100 days, and of this number Governor Brough pledged the Buckeye State for 30,000. The tender was accepted troops to be mustered into service by regiments to be filled up according regulations as to the minimum strength, organized according to the regulations of the War Department, all to be furnished within twenty days from acceptance armed, equipped, etc., and paid as other United States infantry volunteers, to serve wherever their services were required, no bounty to be paid these troops.

Immediately upon the acceptance Governor Brough telegraphed B. R. Cowen, Adjutant General, to set the machinery in motion and on Monday morning, April 25, the press throughout the state published the following:

GENERAL HEADQUARTERS, STATE OF OHIO,
ADJUTANT-GENERAL'S OFFICE,
COLUMBUS, April 25, 1864.

General Order No. 12.

The regiments, battalions and independent companies of infantry of the National Guard of Ohio, are hereby called into active service for the term of one hundred days unless sooner discharged. They will be clothed, armed, equipped, transported and paid by the United States Government.

These organizations will rendezvous at the most eligible places in their respective counties (the place to be fixed by the commanding officer and to be on a line of railroad if practicable) on Monday, May 2d, 1864, and report by telegraph at 4 o'clock P. M. of same day, the number present for duty.

The alacrity with which all calls for the military of the state have been heretofore met furnishes the surest guaranty that the National Guard will be prompt to assemble at the appointed time.

Our armies in the field are marshaling for a decisive blow, and the citizen soldiery will share the glory of the crowning victories of the campaign, by relieving our valiant regiments from post and garrison duty to allow them to engage in the more arduous labors of the field.

By order of the Governor.

R. B. COWEN,
Adjutant General.

The day arrived for the mustering at their respective rendezvous. Before the hour named for report, dispatches came in and at 7 o'clock the Adjutant General telegraphed Secretary Stanton. "More than thirty thousand National Guards in camp and ready for muster, and at 9:30 o'clock the report showed thirty-eight thousand men in camp clamorous to be sent forward.

Of the whole volunteer militia of the state but one company (Company B, 40th Battalion, Captain Wendell Mischler) refused to obey the order calling it out, and at once under special order No. 374 by order of the Governor was dishonorably dismissed from the service of the State of Ohio.

The labor of consolidation was difficult owing to thousands of the original members having entered the national service. Every regiment was reduced low the minimum, but army officers of experience were called to aid and the principle adopted was to break up the smaller organizations and divide the men in such proportions as were needed.

CHAPTER II.

GATHERING OF THE BOYS.—Immediately upon receipt of the Adjutant General's order, Colonel Innis forwarded copies of it to the Captains of the Companies composing the Third Regiment Ohio Volunteer Militia, and with it his order designating the hall of Company B. (Meade Rifles) in the Carpenter block on Town street between Third and Fourth as the place of meeting, and 7 o'clock A. M. as the time.

Promptly at the hour the men began to pour in. The companies from outside the city came in wagons with their fifes screaming, drums beating vigorously, and flags flying, giving spectators the impression that they were full of martial spirit and ready to meet the enemy at once.

The feeling seemed to be that we were called for a special purpose and that the emergency was something beyond any which had yet presented itself, and all seemed to feel the importance of it.

Soon the whole regiment was gathered at headquarters and speculation was rife as to where we were to be sent.

Of course we could only guess, and this we did to the best of our ability all day, starting anew at every rumor that came to our ears.

During the day quite a number of members of

the regiment who thought they could not go, or who disliked the idea of going, secured substitutes at some price or other, many agreeing to give their representatives a dollar a day while in the service, besides their pay from the government.

Thus the day passed and at 6 P. M. companies A. and B. being composed entirely of men who lived in the city were dismissed for the night, but with strict orders to report at 7 o'clock in the morning or be considered deserters. The balance of the regiment was marched to Tod Barracks just north of the present Union Depot, where the Columbus Buggy Co's lumber yard now is.

Here all was hurry and bustle, drums were beating provost squads coming and going, and soldiers in their blue uniforms moving about the enclosure which seemed to fairly swarm with them. All this was new to our unprepared minds, but it was the beginning of our soldier education. Once inside the gate the boys were under more restraint than they had ever been used to, and although many of them desired to step outside for a little while to secure additional articles of baggage, or make final arrangement of their business, the guard was an obstacle which could not be surmounted.

They all yielded gracefully after doing a little grumbling, which they considered a soldiers privilege.

SOLDIER FARE.—About the first thing to be thought of was supper, so some of the hungry ones made an excursion to the cook shanties at the rear of the camp to investigate.

On their return the report was: Gewhillikins, boys! you ought to see the stuff they are dishing out to those old soldiers. Wonder if we'll get the same! By golly, I can't eat that greasy sowbelly, and those beans cooked in that dirty kettle smoked all up so; the hard-tack looks like chips and there is no butter to put on it, and the coffee is black and they get it in old dirty tincups. I guess I'll go home.

So they rattled on, and really, not many cared for supper that night although some professed to be well satisfied. As night came on we realized that we must find some place to sleep, though the very thought of passing the night in such quarters seemed repugnant. We thought of the great numbers of soldiers, some of them not very cleanly, who had been quartered here, and we were suspicious that the bunks were already occupied by those very interesting little insects that accompany the soldier through his service unless he takes extra precautions to keep rid of them, and the thought was anything but pleasurable.

USEFUL HINTS. — The old soldiers were friendly in giving us advice as to how "to git rid of 'em". "Soak your clothes in strong salt water," or "Boil your clothes, that'll knock 'em," all of which advice we treasured up for future use.

The different companies selected their bunks, which were in tiers at the sides of the large frame buildings, each bunk being about four feet wide and the length of a man. The bedding was nowhere to be found, so each man had to spread his coat or whatever he happened to have with him, on the bare boards and use his spare pair of socks for a pillow.

They declared that this was better than the indian's feather-bed, which consisted of one feather on a rock. After they were comfortably settled it was announced that we had taken some other regiment's quarters, and so we had to get out at 10 P. M. and go to another building no better furnished.

Here we failed to find sleep, owing to the continual noise of goers and comers added to the hullabaloo kept up by some of the lively members of our regiment. At 4 A. M. we gave up trying to sleep and got out to saunter around the camp and straighten out the kinks in our bodies and rub the sore spots caused by the pressure of our downy couches. At 5 A. M. the reveille sounded, when all were supposed to rise and prepare for breakfast. If any one was slow about rising he was sure of plenty of assistance from his bunkmates.

The facilities for morning ablutions consisted of wetting the hands at the pump, a swipe or two at the face, and then drying them on whatever was handy, from a blouse sleeve or handkerchief to a newspaper or the tail of a shirt.

Breakfast was the same as last night's supper, though it seemed a little better owing to the growing appetites.

Being unorganized we had no duty to perform, so we spent the day lying in our bunks, or reading, singing or lounging around the barracks. In the meantime a few absentees were sent for and brought in.

A physical examination of the members of the regiment who claimed to be unfitted for service, was conducted by the surgeons in a hurried way and did not exclude many from service. One man who succeeded in getting excused from service by the surgeons and reported to the Colonel for his approval, said: "Colonel, I have no doubt I could stand the service as well as any of the men, but the fact is my family cannot get along without me, and my business will suffer, this is why I got excused."

The Colonel answered: "My dear sir! I cannot approve of your being excused, for you are no worse off than the most of the members of the regiment. They are also leaving their business suddenly, and their families unprovided for, yet they go cheerfully when called. And *he* went.

A supplementary examination was made after reaching Camp Chase to determine the condition of teeth and eyes. None were excluded at this examination.

It was not known this morning what would be done with us, so the boys again put in their time guessing where we were to go.

CAMP CHASE.—In the morning (May 5th) the guessing continued and the probability that we were to be sent to the Kanawha Valley seemed to increase. During the forenoon orders came for us to march to Camp Chase. At 2 P. M. we took up our line of march and after a hot, dusty tramp of five miles reached our destination. Here we found the ground had been cleared by a detail which had been sent ahead for the purpose. Pitching tents was a trick which the boys had to learn, but fortunately some few of them had had a taste of service, and under their direction we were under cover and got supper by nine o'clock.

NEW BEDS.—Sleeping on the ground was a new experience with most of us, but the boys took hold with a determination to do their part cheerfully and although next morning there were many aching bones nobody complained.

Our orders were to perfect the organization of the regiment as quickly as possible, that we were needed immediately. Two telegrams were sent to Governor Brough by the Secretary of War. The first read, "Has Ohio a regiment that can be sent at once to West Virginia? It is needed badly."

This was followed by a second which read, "For God's sake hurry up and send a regiment. The rebels are threatening our stores at New Creek."

CHAPTER III.

HOW THE REGIMENT WAS MADE UP.—
The regiment was filled up by adding two companies of the 76th Battalion O. N. G. from Franklin County, and two companies of the 58th Battalion O. N. G. from Hancock County to the 3rd Regiment O. N. G. from Franklin County. This work of consolidation was done by the regimental officers without assistance, and was the only hundred days regiment whose officers performed that duty.

Numerous changes were necessary before everything was satisfactorily adjusted. There was an excess of officers after the organization of the new regiment. This was arranged for the most part among the officers themselves, but in a few instances choice was made by the men.

The Captains of the absorbed battalions accepted First Lieutenants commissions. Some of the First Lieutenants became Second Lieutenants, and those who did not get places remained at home, except two lieutenants who enlisted and served as privates. One of these was Second Lieutenant Eli White of Company F. 3d O. N. G. These changes made it rather unpleasant for the men, for being transferred in small numbers to other companies it separated them from companions with whom they had enlisted, and with whom they expected to mess and bunk. But they were men of intelligence and did not need to have the necessity explained to them. They accepted the situation and were soon hail fellows with all.

GOOD MATERIAL.—Right here I may remark that there was no regiment in the army which outranked the 133d in the personal character and intelligence of its members, rank and file. They were of the more substantial class of citizens who having assisted in organizing and supplying all the troops so far sent out, were now in charge of the business of the community, and it was thought they could not be spared. When Morgan raided the state, they organized for home protection and at the call for One Hundred Days they left everything and went forth.

The positions of honor and trust in which the survivors may to-day be found is an indication of the quality of the men.

The mustering in was done in the night of May 6th, by Major Cravens, and was not completed until 4 o'clock on the morning of the 7th, the field officers being mustered last though all was dated May 6th, and when mustered into the service of the United States, the regiment was designated the 133d Ohio Volunteer Infantry.

WE DON THE BLUE.—The uniforming of the regiment was done at night, or rather in the morning of the 7th. The Captain with a detail of half a dozen men would report to the quartermaster the number of men in his company. The proper number of Overcoats, Blouses, Pants, Drawers, Shoes, Socks, etc., were pulled out of boxes and tossed to the men in waiting. When one got all he could carry he would go to company quarters and there each man received his allowance. The matter of a fit was left out of the question by the Quartermaster.

This was fun for the boys. Some of their legs and arms stuck out of the trouser legs and sleeves too far, while others had to roll up both extremities and were then too small to fill the balance of the suit. A system of exchange was instituted by which each one was finally fitted and everyone was happy.

The men were then required to sign the clothing receipt roll, each article being charged in separate columns under appropriate headings.

The prices were:

Hat	$1.65
Pants	2 50
Shirt	1 53
Drawers	90
Socks	32
Shoes	2 48
Overcoat	7 50
Poncho	2 75
Blouse	3 12
Blanket	3 50
Making our clothing cost	$26 25

Before this was finished, urgent orders were received by the Colonel to march at once, that the regiment was badly needed to protect the Baltimore and Ohio R. R., which the rebels were threatening in West Virginia.

Everything was hurly burly. Snatching up their knapsacks and canteens the men fell in, some only partly dressed, and the march was begun at 5 o'clock A. M. to the State Arsenal on West Friend (now Main) street.

THE REGIMENT ARMED.—Here we were each handed a Springfield rifle and the necessary accoutrements, and the non-commissioned officers in addition a straight sword a piece which they called "toad stickers" and "cheese toasters", which they afterward learned were of no earthly use, unless it was to get between their legs when on the double quick.

GOOD BYE.—The friends and relatives had collected and lined the streets as we marched to the depot. Many "good byes" were said and many of the boys looked sadly at the stores and shops along High street where they had been employed and wondered if they would ever take their places in them again.

Just after we arrived at the depot the Colonel was approached by a prominent citizen who requested that one of the men be granted a leave of absence as his mother was very sick, but the Colonel being under imperative orders to march at once could not grant the request and was roundly abused by the citizen.

We were not permitted to lose any time but were loaded into box-cars and were at 11 o'clock A. M. on the way south over the Little Miami R. R. This was pretty quick work, the regiment being mustered, uniformed, armed and equipped for the field, and on the way to the front in less than twelve hours, and was the first of the Hundred Days regiments to leave the state.

Thirty-eight thousand men taken from the working force of the state, after all that had previously enlisted, left very few at home to put in the crops, and attend and harvest them. On many farms the women and children were compelled to do the work, and a man was almost a rarity in some neighborhoods. The following letter of Governor Brough, taken from the "Ohio State Journal" of May 9, 1864, shows something of the situation.

FAMILIES AND CROPS TO BE CARED FOR.

Governor Brough to the People.
Five thousand dollars appropriated to the families of the National Guard. Good suggestion.

Executive Department Ohio.
Columbus, May 9, 1864.

To the Military Committee and People of the State:

The departure of the National Guard from the State, in the service of the country will necessarily work much individual hardship. In many cases in each county, families of laboring men dependent on the daily labor of the head will be left almost wholly unprovided for. The compensation of the soldier will not enable him to provide for the daily wants of his family. We who remain at home, protected by the patriotism and sacrifices of these noble men, must not permit their families to suffer. The prompt response of the Guard to the call has reflected honor upon the State. We must not sully it by neglecting the wants of those our gallant troops leave behind.

No such stain must rest upon the fair character of our people. As organized, is even better than individual action, I suggest to the people of the several counties that they promptly raise by voluntary contribution, a sufficient sum to meet the probable wants of the families of the Guards, who may require aid, and place the same in the hands of the Military Committee of the county, for appropriation and distribution.

The Committee can designate one or two good men in each township, who will cheerfully incur the trouble and labor of passing upon all cases in their townships and of drawing and paying such appropriation as may be made to them. Citizens let this fund be ample. Let those whom God has blessed with abundance contribute it freely. It is not a charity to which you may give grudgingly. It is payment of only part of the debt we all owe the brave men who have responded to the call of the country and whose action is warding off from us deadly perils, and saving us from much more serious sacrifices. What is all your wealth to you if your Government be subverted. What is the value of your stores, if your public credit or finances be ruined or rebel armies invade and traverse your State. Be liberal and generous then in this emergency.

Let no mother, wife, or child of the noble Guard want the comforts of life during the hundred days, and let those noble men feel on their return that the people of the State appreciated, and have to some extent, relieved the sacrifices they so promptly made in the hour of the country's need.

As these families do not come within the means

provided by the Relief Law, we must look to voluntary contributions to provide for them. In aid of these I feel authorized to appropriate the sum of *Five Thousand Dollars* from the military contingent fund. This sum will be apportioned among the several counties in proportion to the number of the Guard drawn from each, and the chairman of the military committee early notified of the amount subject to his order.

In many cases men left crops partly planted, and fields sown, that in due time must be harvested or lost. In each township and county there should be at once associations of men at home who will resolve that to the extent of their ability they will look to these things. It is not only the dictate of patriotism, but of good citizenship that we make an extra exertion to save the crops to the country, and the accruing value to the owners, who, instead of looking to seed-time and harvest, are defending us from invasion and destruction. Men of the cities and towns, when the harvest is ready for the reaper, give a few days of your time and go forth by dozens and fifties to the work. The labor may be severe, but the sacrifice will be small, and the reflection of the good you have done will more than compensate you for it all.

In this contest for the supremacy of our government, and the salvation of our country Ohio occupies a proud position. Her standard must not be lowered; rather let us advance it to the front. No brighter glory can be reflected on it than will result from a prompt and generous support to the families of the Guard. Let us all to the work.

Very respectfully,
JOHN BROUGH.

HOW EQUIPPED.—The uniforming, arming, and equipping was done wholly from the resources already in the state, no requisition being made on the general government for anything. This made the United States Quartermasters Department wonder how it had been done, but Ohio had some good men in charge of her affairs, and also the resources.

All the Hundred Days regiments were equipped in the same way, contrary to the original agreement with the governors.

Two weeks after the last regiment crossed the Ohio River Colonel Burr received a telegram that the government had just shipped two car loads of accoutrements to help equip the Hundred Days regiments.

At Loveland we took the Cincinnati & Marietta R. R., which conveyed us to Belpre, twelve miles south of Marietta. All along the route we were welcomed by the people with hearty cheers. This was our first Sunday in the service, but it did not seem at all like Sunday. Gliding along the railroad in box-cars, cheered by the people, no religious service, and thinking all the time that we would soon be facing the enemy, robbed the day of its religious character. At Belpre we went on board a steamboat which carried us across the river to Parkersburg at two trips.

While waiting for the boat the boys had to draw on their haversacks where they had been required to deposit three days rations before starting from Camp Chase.

The fat pork and hard-tack were now brought out and devoured with considerable satisfaction, even by those who at first thought they never could eat such stuff.

The bounty jumpers who infested the army did not fail to take advantage of the bounty offered by those who sent substitutes in the 133d, and having secured their money, three of them deserted from Company H. before we reached the Ohio River.

At Parkersburg we went into camp about noon, put up our dog-tents, and remained until Tuesday morning.

CHAPTER IV.

NO YANKEES NEED APPLY.—In establishing the guard lines a large farm house near the camp was pretty thoroughly protected. The Colonel and other officers applied at this house for supper, but were told that they did not propose to wait on Yanks although the officers observed that they were well supplied with provisions and plenty of poultry. Finding they were rebel sympathizers, the guard lines were changed somewhat, and the boys having found that the poultry was first class eating were not slow to appropriate all they could reach.

After establishing our camp, ten rounds of ammunition was issued to us, and after battalion drill the boys were taken out to try their guns. Although most of them knew which end of the weapon was to be pointed toward the enemy, some very laughable ignorance in the use of firearms was displayed. After dark, when about retiring beneath our shelter tents for the night, it was whispered about that there were spies in camp, and we were warned to look out for strangers.

HE WAS AFRAID OF WAR.—It developed that a man had been arrested in Parkersburg in the act of changing his uniform for citizens clothing, having the latter partly on, with the uniform lying by. He was brought before the regimental officers, who recognized him as a soldier who had been sworn in by the name of Robert G. Forgrave, Sergeant of Company F., though that was not his real name. He confessed that he was about to desert, and after being told that any further attempt in that direction would be punished by prompt execution, he was allowed to again take his place in his company. He made no further attempt to desert, but was on July 31st reduced to ranks for cowardice. During the fight at Ware Bottom Church, Forgrave was found missing. A soldier reported that a pair of boots was protruding from under a brushheap. On pulling them out they were found to be occupied by Forgrave.

HIS ARDOR DAMPENED.—After trying our guns, squad drill was indulged in. The ground was quite level and nice to drill on, except where some large trees had been blown down. Where the roots were torn out there would be quite a hole. These holes were filled with water with leaves floating on the surface.

A pompous little dutch sergeant who was drilling a squad and walking backward failed to observe the location of one of these holes, a good deep one, and in a twinkling disappeared from view. He presently floundered out, soaked from head to foot, minus his pomposity and spluttering something worse than German.

The affair was so ludicrous, and the audience so appreciative, that the drill closed at once.

GOOD NEWS.—While here we received news that Grant had outflanked Lee and forced him to retreat. This news was received with great enthusiasm, and the camp resounded with three hearty cheers by the whole regiment. Our baggage arrived some time after the regiment got into camp, but in such a mixed up mess that no one could tell where his own property was. Some in despair took what they could get. This led to charges of stealing, but finally the muddle was cleared up and every man got his own. Several boxes of clothing and other articles that the boys found they could get along without, were shipped home from this place.

WE MOVE ON.—On the morning of the 10th, at 4 o'clock, we were ordered to strike tents, pack up, get our breakfast and be ready to march.

We took the cars (cattle cars) at 8 o'clock, with orders to proceed to New Creek, W. Va, a Baltimore and Ohio railroad station on the north branch of the Potomac, where the government had a large amount of ammunition and supplies which the rebels were threatening.

Things began to look as though we were soldiering in earnest, but no one flinched. The scenery along the railroad is wild and romantic, among the mountains, along the sides of ravines, with a hill hundreds of feet high on one side and a hollow as deep on the other with the stream at the bottom looking like a silver ribbon. A fellow could not help thinking, What if the train should tilt off the little shelf where the track was laid? What would become of us? There were a great many tunnels along the route, some of them very long. At one place a tunnel had given way, and we were delayed an hour or more at Clarksburg till it could be repaired. A cold rain began in the evening, and this, together with the fact that the cattle cars were not clean nor provided with seats, made the night a very uncomfortable one, but on and on we went, sometimes sidetracking to let trains pass, then on again through the cold rain, no chance to make coffee nor cook breakfast, nor dry ourselves.

For breakfast we had to reach into our haversacks and pull out our cold boiled fat meat and hardtack, and we were hungry enough to eat them. In the forenoon the drivingrod of the engine pulling the rear section of the train, conveying most of the officers, broke, and that part of the regiment was delayed three hours. The engineer managed to fix his engine up so we could go on, though in a crippled condition.

THE BOYS WERE READY TO MEET THE REBS.—Near Moorefild the train was stopped and a hundred men called for to go ahead where some guerrillas were reported to be. The whole regiment stepped forward, but as all were not needed a hundred were detailed and went forward for some distance, till they met a train coming our way and learned that there were no rebels to be seen. The crippled engine again went on with us through the rainy night. In the morning, May 11th, when we arrived at Piedmont, we found that the rebels had destroyed the little town, burned the railroad shops and taken a small amount of military stores.

This happened last Thursday, the day we marched to Camp Chase.

This was the first glimpse we had of the realities of war.

NEW CREEK.—Five miles further on we reached our destination, New Creek, and marched across an open field to comfortable huts built of small pine logs, in each of which were bunks for twelve or fourteen men. They were on the bottom land along the south side of the Potomac, which is the boundary line between Virginia and Maryland. The open field between these huts and the railroad was the parade ground.

There being cabins enough for only four or five companies the rest pitched their tents on the hill just outside the fort.

Mountains are on every side, and every little cloud that floats by seems charged with rain, but the soil is sandy and soon absorbs all the water that falls.

AN ALARM.—We cleaned up our quarters and got supper, but had no more than eaten it till we were ordered immediately to the fort on the top of a large hill to the southwest of the village. This fort (Fort Fuller) was built by Stonewall Jackson, but he was shelled out of it by General Fremont who planted his artillery on the top of the high hill just north of the river, since which it has been occupied by union forces. We were informed that an attack by the rebel general Imboden's forces was momentarily expected, as the scouts reported him only three miles off. Forty rounds of amunition was issued to each man and we marched up the hill and into the fort.

There was a little redoubt about a quarter of a mile to the northwest of the fort, which it was necessary to occupy with a company as a sort of strong picket or advance post. It was situated at the end of the ridge or hill on which the fort was, and along the road by which the enemy would come in making an attack.

Colonel Innis came down the line with a lantern asking for a company to take this post, but it did not seem desirable. Coming to Company H. he asked Captain Williams if he would like to take the place.

Turning to his men the Captain asked, How is it, men? Do we want to go out there where the rebs will find us first?

Yes, yes! came the answer, anywhere out of this mud. So Company H. marched out there and after the danger of attack was over and their camp fixed up a little they found it a very pleasant place. Afterward Company I. camped between them and the fort, and both companies remained there until we left New Creek.

Here we lay on our arms in the mud and rain catching snatches of sleep as we could, which was very little indeed. At 3 o'clock in the morning we were routed out and formed in line ready for an attack. This was caused by a picket firing at some object moving in the dark which did not respond to his challange. The rebels did not appear and scouts brought in word that they had retreated.

HARD WORK.—The men were pretty well worn out by this time, having been two days and one night on the comfortless cars with the cold rain beating in on them, and last night still worse in the mud and water from four to eight inches deep.

May 12th, about ten o'clock, a part of the regiment was allowed to go down to our quarters and do some cooking.

So many men are necessary for picket and guard duty that after drilling each day not much time is got for rest, and the boys think they are seeing hard service.

WE SAVE MONEY FOR UNCLE SAM.—We now realize how necessary it was for our regiment to get here, for the government has stores here to the amount of several millions of dollars, and only a few troops to guard them. This was very tempting to the rebels who were hovering about awaiting a favorable moment to attack the place and capture the supplies.

Fort Fuller was not large enough to allow all the men at the breastworks at once, so about one-third of them who were considered the best marksmen, were placed in front to do the shooting and the rest were to do the loading. But happily the news of our arrival reached the rebel general and he found it expedient to retire.

The regiment arriving in two sections three hours apart, led the rebels to believe that two regiments had arrived, and when the companies from the log huts marched up to the fort they thought there was still another, making it appear that very strong reinforcements had been received.

Thus the timely arrival of the 133d saved the United States millions of dollars.

The men felt very much elated over having scared the enemy off, though some seemed quite disappointed that the rebels did not attack us, fully believing that we should have licked them.

But some would have lost their lives so it was best that it turned out as it did.

STEADY DRILL.—We now put in all our spare time drilling, squad, company, and battalion drill, and soon we were quite well up in the different movements. Duties became regular.

Reveille	5:00 A. M.
Roll call	5:30 A. M.
Breakfast	6:00 A. M.
Sick call	7:00 A. M.
Guard detail	7:30 A. M.
Guard mounting	8:00 A. M.
Squad drill	9:00 A. M.
Company drill	10:00 A. M.
Dinner	12:00 M.
Battalion drill	2:00 P. M.
Dress parade	5:00 P. M.

The fife and drum at Reveille was supposed to wake every one in camp, and the boys would come tumbling out of their bunks rubbing the lame places caused by lying on the boughs of trees which they had placed to keep them off the ground. Very fortunate were they if they had boards to lie on. If any were dilatory about rising they were pretty sure to be assisted by their messmates.

When all were up and dressed they would form in line in the street between the two rows of tents which the company occupied, and the orderly sergeant would call the roll, each one answering to his name, or if on guard or sick be so reported. The orderly would then report to the captain that all were present or accounted for, and the company would be dismissed for breakfast. An hour was given for this meal and cleaning up the quarters. At the sick call all who were ailing or claimed to be (for some played off sick) were formed in line, the orderly made a note of them and sent them in charge of a sergeant or corporal to the surgeon's tent, or hospital tent, where they were prescribed for and excused from duty, or reported able for duty as the case required. Then came guard detail and guard mounting. The orderly sergeant of each company would name a certain number of men (designated by the adjutant) taking them in rotation from his company roll, usually ten or more.

These several details would be marched to the parade grounds and there formed in line, when the adjutant would put them through a few evolutions, marching in review, and then send them to their different posts, some on guard around camp, some on picket posts two or three miles out on the different roads by which an enemy might approach.

Now came the *work* of the day, drilling. At 9 o'clock the men were formed into squads of eight to twelve men and put through the different movements, facing, marching, etc., with and without arms, being under the command of a lieutenant or non-commissioned officer.

When this had lasted for an hour, the squads were united into companies and the captain or a lieutenant would drill them together for two hours, marching by flank, wheeling by company, forming sections and platoons, and in the manual of arms.

This was pretty tiresome work, and the men were glad when they were dismissed for dinner at nearly noon. After resting until 2 o'clock, the companies were again formed and marched to the parade ground, two or more companies uniting into battalions, when they were drilled by the field officers or a captain acting as major. Finally all were united and drilled as a regiment in similar movements, only on a larger scale.

DRESS PARADE.—The regiment was dismissed in time to slick up a little for dress parade at 5 o'clock. This was a ceremonious affair, every one being supposed to have on his clean clothes, or at least to have his only suit brushed, shoes blackened, guns and acoutrements polished, so as to present as respectable an appearance as possible.

For fear the boys have forgotten in the thirty years or more that have since passed how it was done, the following description of dress parade is given from U. S. Army Regulations of that date.

"A signal will be beat or sounded (on bugle) half an hour before *troop* or *retreat* for the music to assemble on the regimental parade and each company to turn out under arms on its own parade (street) for roll call and inspection by its own officers.

Ten minutes after that signal, the *Adjutants call* will be given, when the captains will march their companies (the band playing) to the regimental parade, where they take their positions in the order of battle. When the line is formed the captain of the first company, on notice from the Adjutant, steps one pace to the front and gives to his company the command

Order ARMS. PARADE REST.

which is repeated by each captain in succession to the left.

The Adjutant takes post two paces on the right of the line, the Sergeant Major two paces on the left. The music will be formed in two ranks on the right of the Adjutant. The senior officer present will take command of the parade and will take post at a suitable distance in front opposite the centre, facing the line. When the companies have ordered arms, the Adjutant will order the music to *beat off*, when it will commence on the right, beat in front of the line to the left, and back to its place on the right. When the music has ceased the Adjutant will step two paces to the front, face to the left and command, *Attention!* *Battalion!* *Shoulder arms!* *Prepare to open ranks!* *To the rear open order!* March!

At the sixth command the ranks will be opened by the rear rank taking four paces to the rear, the commissioned officers marching to the front, the company officers four paces, the field officers six paces opposite to their positions in the order of battle, where they will halt and dress.

The Adjutant seeing the ranks aligned will command, *Present* ARMS! when arms will be presented, the officers saluting. Seeing this executed he will face about to the commanding officer, salute, and report, *Sir, the parade is formed.*

The Adjutant will then, on intimation to that

effect, take his station three paces on the left of the commanding officer, one pace retired, passing round his rear.

The commanding officer having acknowledged the salute of the line by touching his hat, will, after the Adjutant has taken his post, draw his sword and command, *Battalion Shoulder* ARMS! and add such exercises as he may think proper, concluding with *Order* ARMS! then return his sword and direct the Adjutant to receive reports. The Adjutant will now pass round the right of the commanding officer, advance upon the line, halt midway between him and the line of company officers and command, *First Sergeants to the front and centre.* MARCH!

At the first command they will *shoulder arms* as Sergeants, march two paces to the front and face inward. At the second command they will march to the centre and halt. The Adjutant will then order, *Front Face! Report!*

At the last word each in succession, beginning on the right, will salute by bringing the left hand smartly across the breast to the right shoulder and report the result of the roll call previously made on the company parade.

The Adjutant again commands, *First Sergeants, outward* FACE! *To your posts!* MARCH! when they will resume their places and order arms. The Adjutant will now face to the commanding officer, salute, report absent officers and give the result of the First Sergeant's reports.

The commanding officer will next direct the orders to be read, when the Adjutant will face about and announce, *Attention to Orders!* He will then read the orders. The orders having been read, the Adjutnat will face to the commanding officer, salute, and report, when, on an intimation from the commander, he will face again to the line and announce, *Parade is dismissed.* All the officers will now return their swords, face inward, and close on the Adjutant, he having taken position in their line, the field officers on the flanks. The Adjutant commands, *Front Face! Forward, March!* when they will march forward, dressing on the centre, the music playing, and when within six paces of the commander, the Adjutant will give the word *Halt!*

The officers will then salute the commanding officer by raising the hand to the cap, and there remain until he shall have communicated to them such instructions as he shall have to give, or intimates that the ceremony is finished.

As the officers disperse, the First Sergeant s will close the ranks of their respective companies and march them to the company parade, where they will be dismissed, the band continuing to play until the companies clear the regimental parade."

One occasion while on dress parade, our band was so convulsed with laughter that for a moment or two the music was spasmodic and out of time. The cause was that our bass drummer while passing the front of the regiment, stepped into a small ditch which ran through the parade ground. His big drum being before him he could not see the ditch and was entirely unprepared for the movement he executed. When he reached the spot, the drum went down to the ground, there was a twinkling of heels in the air and the drummer found he had turned a complete summersault over his instrument.

As might be expected, there were a thousand smiles on the parade ground, some of them pretty loud.

Dress parade concluded the days work for those in camp. Supper was usually ready when the companies were dismissed and the men hastened to dispose of it.

There would then be two or three hours before evening roll call, which would be spent in washing or mending clothes, cleaning guns and acoutrements, writing letters and diaries, visiting about camp, etc.

At 9 o'clock the company fell in for evening roll call, when all must be accounted for again. Then at 9:30 taps were sounded, lights put out, and silence held sway for the night.

Such was the routine of a soldiers life when doing garrison duty, or when in camp where the duties were not too active. Of course when in the presence of or in close proximity to the enemy, the ceremonious parts were left out, and only the necessary duties performed.

CHAPTER V.

SUPPLYING OUTPOSTS.—About twice a week a wagon-train bearing supplies of ammunition and provisions for the forces guarding Greenland Gap and other posts was sent out from this place.

The Gap is twenty-two miles south of New Creek, is two hundred feet wide, with hills eleven hundred feet high on each side, and is guarded by five hundred men. These trains were usualy guarded by one hundred and fifty or two hundred men under a captain and lieutenants, who went out one day and returned the next, but sometimes started back the same day they got there and camped along the way.

So matters went on, the weather was rainy most of the time, but there were some pleasant days when it only rained five or six times a day.

ABOVE THE CLOUDS.—Sometimes we would see down the valleys what appeared to be smoke, and when we asked a native what that fire was, were laughingly told that it was a thunder shower away below us. We soon found that this was true. They were clouds.

PICKET DUTY.—Picket duty was especially unpleasant. The men had to stay on their posts two or three miles from camp in the ravines where there were wagon roads for twenty-four hours at a time, and get wet through four or five times as the showers passed by.

As soon as night came on the Whip-poor-wills set up their cry in the bushes and kept it up till daylight, making it more lonesome than ever. The guards were divided as is usual into three reliefs, with two hours on and four hours off duty, so that a fellow could get a couple of naps during the night, if he attended strictly to business and went directly to sleep, except when it was raining, and then it takes a mighty tired man to sleep with the rain splashing in his face or trickling down his back. Sometimes wild deer are seen by the pickets, and bear and other game are reported rather plenty.

SAUCY REBELS.—The men carried one days rations with them when they went on picket, and sometimes could add a little extra, as berries, roasting ears, potatoes, etc. And then, once in a while, a pig or chicken would come up, and in the most tantalizing manner hurrah for the Southern Confederacy, right before their faces.

Of course every soldier was sworn to do all in his power to suppress the rebellion, and the 133d was deeply impressed with this duty, therefore, when any animal had the impudence to act that way, it was at once suppressed, and effectually, too.

In some localities stringent rules were laid down against foraging, and the boys who did not heed them, ran risks of punishment.

HIGH PRICED PORK.—On one of these posts, several miles from New Creek, was a detail of very young boys, among the rest one who has since become prominent in state politics, has filled a state office with marked ability, and been prominently mentioned for governor. A fine sow and pigs came about their post and brought memories of roast pig and such things to their minds.

The more they tried to resist the temptation, the stronger it grew, and the more saucy the rebel pigs became. At last the boys could stand it no longer and took after the porkers. Up and down, and around and around they ran until finally one succeeded in thrusting his bayonet through the fattest one, (they dared not shoot, as that was the signal of an attack). They skinned the little fellow, roasted him nicely, and soon the stomachs of the picket squad were feeling more comfortable than for a long time. They destroyed all evidence of the slaughter and agreed to keep mum.

After a while an Irishman came to the boys and said he was looking for a lost pig. He had eight, and now there were only seven. The innocent boys helped him hunt in the neighborhood. They had noticed a sow about there, but there were only seven pigs with her when they saw them. The Irishman went away and the boys snickered quietly.

Next morning when they returned to camp and were dismissed from duty they were ordered to report at headquarters. The Irishman had been there and entered complaint of his loss. The pickets were called in one at a time and questioned, but each denied all knowledge of the lost pig until one, worse scared than the rest, gave up the secret. Each one was assessed three dollars and Pat was paid in full.

RELIGIOUS SERVICES.—May 15th was Sunday, and our chaplain gave us a good sermon, most of the boys attending. Some of the more religiously inclined hold prayer meetings in their quarters at night.

Having no meeting house with us, we had to sit on logs, rocks and stumps, or lie on the ground, or stand around during preaching. When it came to the hymns, nearly everyone joined in singing them, and it was not such bad music that we made either.

Two regiments of One Hundred Days men, the 152d and 154th, came in to-day, and camped on the ground just west of us along the creek, being over a week behind us. The ground where they camped is almost covered with water from the constant rains. The creek is not very large here, and the water is usually clear and blue as it goes tumbling along over the rocks, there being a great deal of fall here among the mountains, but now it is quite muddy and swollen, and runs very swiftly. There are a few places thirty or forty yards long where the creek is level, and these make delightful swimming places, as well as good places in which to wash our clothes.

The pioneer corps is building a foot-bridge across the creek, of logs supported on trestles. They just wade through the water up to their breasts, with their clothes on, utterly regardless of the wetting they get.

OUR FRIENDS ALARMED.—A report has reached home that the 133d has been all cut to pieces, and Dr. Guerin has been sent on to ascertain the facts. He was happily disappointed to find the report false, and the boys in good shape and fast becoming used to the business of soldiering. He at once sent home the comforting news and our friends were relieved of their anxiety. A good many soldiers pass over the railroad both ways, this being the nearest line between the eastern and western theatres of war.

ANOTHER SCARE.—On the night of the 21st there were rumors of an attack and we were routed out at midnight, and lay on our arms till morning. On the 22d the lookouts on Mount Piano reported a rebel camp in view ten miles off.

Scouts were sent out to ascertain the facts, but before their return it was decided that an orchard in bloom had deceived the lookouts, and there was no rebel camp near.

The weather has now become more pleasant and admits of steady work at drilling, the days are quite hot and the nights cool. The letters which reach us from home help to cheer the boys up and keep them in good spirits.

On Monday, May 23d, we were given three rounds of cartridges at battalion drill, and tried our marksmanship on some trees and stumps. The firing at command and accuracy of aim were quite creditable.

COPPERHEADS.—To-day news was received that Sam Medary, editor of "The Crisis", at Columbus, was arrested for treason. To-night a meeting was held and several stirring, patriotic speeches made by different members of the regiment. Vigorous language was used in regard to the traitorous utterances of "The Crisis", but all had full faith that the people at home would manage the copperheads around them.

Some of the men have formed a club and subscribed for the "Ohio State Journal", and this, with the papers sent by friends, keeps us posted on events at home and in the army. Grant has been doing terrible fighting with Lee, and although he has lost very heavily, the advantage is with the Union Army.

AT FEARFUL COST.—On the 24th of May news came that Grant had whipped Lee badly, and he was falling back on Richmond. This is good news, but the Union loss since May 1st is terrible. It is stated to be forty thousand.

This seems a fearful sacrifice. Just think! Forty regiments like ours. It is awful! And yet, this is only a small portion of the waste of human life in order to save the Union. And no one can tell when it will end, nor who will be left to enjoy the fruits of victory. Many rebel deserters are coming into our camp, and seem very glad to escape from service in the rebel army. They are all required to take the oath of allegiance to the United States. They then leave for the west, most of them for Ohio. Some of them, however, enlist in the Union Army.

One of them made boasts of how he had used Union prisoners. He tried to get away, but was caught and put in irons and bucked and gagged, to give him a taste of his own medicine.

They are from different parts of the Confederacy and show signs of hard living, so one does not wonder that they desert.

On May 29th the 154th O. V. I. went down to

Greenland Gap and relieved the 2d Maryland, which came into New Creek to take the cars. The 152d O. V. I. was also sent east, and felt very hard that our regiment should be left to do guard duty while they went to the front. Some of them began burning the boards they had floored their tents with, so that we could not have the use of them, but our commander soon convinced them that they were sent to protect "Uncle Sam's" property, instead of to destroy it.

On May 30th the brass band of the 2d Maryland Regiment played for us at dress parade, before leaving for the east.

TO THE RESCUE.—On the afternoon of May 31st a report was received that Captain Williams, who went with the provision train to Greenland Gap this morning, had been attacked. A force of two hundred men was at once sent out to assist him. They got started about 6 o'clock, Captain Steely in command.

Their guide had some difficulty in finding the way and they finally camped for the night. At daylight they got breakfast, and after diligent inquiry found their way to Dull's Gap. Here they found neither our troops nor rebels. The cavalry scouts discovered some of the enemy, but so far off as to be out of reach of our infantry. Captain Williams kept some scouts out and they found a courier in a cabin who was very badly wounded. He was one of two who were carrying dispatches when shot. The other one was killed.

The wounded man was brought into camp, although it was feared he could not live. He was kindly cared for by our surgeons and left in the hospital. We never heard whether he got well or not.

About three o'clock the command started for camp and when within nine miles of New Creek fell in with Captain William's party returning from Greenland Gap. The meeting of the two detachments came near resulting in a tragedy.

A JOKE THAT NEARLY PROVED SERIOUS.—It seems that Captain Steely's party thought to have a little fun at the expense of the other party. They therefore concealed themselves among the bushes on the hill at the side of the road. When the approaching party got opposite them they were startled by the command, Halt! you Yankee sons of b——. Glancing up the hill Captain Williams could see some mysterious movements among the bushes, and naturally supposing there were rebs there quickly brought his men to the side of the train along the fence.

He said, Boys, we can't see them, but we will rake the hill. Ready! and the guns were cocked. At this instant they were surprised to see a Union officer jump up, wave his arms frantically, and cry out, Hold on! For God's sake, Captain, don't shoot! He was not an instant too soon, for within two seconds the commands, Aim! Fire! would have been given, and almost to a certainty some of our men would have been killed and wounded. Moral: Don't fool with men when they are on business.

Neither party had seen any rebels, except thirteen prisoners who were turned over to them at the

Gap, and whom they brought with them. All reached camp about 9 o'clock P. M., June 1st, very tired.

During the march some of the boys got very tired and even gave out. They would not have been able to go on but for the kindness of the Captain and the other mounted officers.

They of course got tired of riding and enjoyed a little walking. They took the boys who were most fatigued and put them on their horses, and after a ride they would feel rested and able to march a while longer.

The boys were very grateful to the officers for thoughtful kindness.

MEASELS and Mumps get us.—During the latter part of May and first part of June quite a good many of the men were sick with measles and mumps, and our surgeons found their hands full. The diseases were very severe with some, and one man (Martin Spangler of Company G.) died from the effects of mumps after reaching Fort Powhatan from which point he was sent to Fortress Monroe.

CHAPTER VI.

AS GOOD AS ANY.—Time would have hung heavy on our hands, had it not been for the everlasting drill and guard duty and even that began to get tiresome.

Our Colonel was desirous that his regiment should be proficient in the drill and all the duties of a soldier, and spared no pains to bring about that condition.

That he succeeded no one will deny and the compliments paid the regiment by the veteran officers under whose command it was placed, proved it conclusively.

A reviewing officer (a West Pointer) Colonel Hoy, from General Siegel's staff visited New Creek on an inspection tour during the latter part of May.

The 133d was inspected by him and he asked Colonel. How long has your regiment been out? Not quite a month. Well *you* have been in the service before. No Sir! Why! I am surprised. They march like old veterans. I have reviewed all the troops in West Virginia and the 133d is unexcelled by any.

Even in the midst of the engagement at Wane Bottom Church although they at first gave way for a little while, they rallied and performed evolutions with the coolness and precision of dress parade calling forth the commendations of Col. J. B. Howell our brigade commander.

Colonel Hoy was a genial Irish gentleman although somewhat profane at times when excited. He remained two or three days and gave us some important lessons in brigade drill.

AFTER GUERRILLAS.—On June 4th about five o'clock in the afternoon the Provost Marshall called for three hundred men from the regiment to go on a scout in the direction of Mechanic's Gap about twenty-eight miles from New Creek where McCausland's guerrillas were supposed to be.

This took all the well men in the regiment who were not on duty.

Two pieces of artillery were attached to the command and all placed under Captain Steely with Captain Fisher ranking next. Three days rations were placed in one haversack and all placed in light marching order with forty rounds of ammunition in our cartridge boxes.

The march was begun and continued most of the night, stopping to reconnoitre at two or three places and finally to await the coming of daylight.

In the morning Lieutenant Parsons with forty men was detached from the command and ordered to go to Dull's Gap, where he would remain three days and then return to camp.

The reason for this was that General Kelly was after McCauslands band of guerrillas and thought they might attempt to pass that way, and the general wished to have all avenues of escape cut off.

The rest of the command pushed on and reached Mechanics Gap about eight o'clock.

The cannon were placed so as to command the

gap and guards stationed at prominent points. The village contained a couple of stores, a church, hotel etc.

The hotel was taken for headquarters and no one allowed to leave. All who came into the village, were detained at the hotel until we left. They were very indignant at this, claiming that they had only come to church which was undoubtedly true of the majority of them but Captain Fisher who had been left in command explained to them that we were in the enemy's country and did not know them, that if they were allowed to depart they might inform the rebels as to our strength, position etc. and bring them upon us, so that while it was an inconvenience to them the circumstances of war made it necessary. The boys looked around the neighborhood and succeeded in *buying* (on credit) and *borrowing* some things to add to the culinary department such as ham, eggs, cornmeal, molasses, honey, potatoes etc. Some of the officers and men went to houses close by and got the folks to provide them with dinner for which they paid. After five or six hours waiting our scouts brought in word that the rebels had taken another direction and left the vicinity.

On a hill quite a distance off was seen some person who it was thought might be one of the enemy's scouts. So a soldier, John Mohr was ordered to fire a shot at him. This he did without any seeming effect, and after half an hour the person fired at came up to us and proved to be a boy fourteen years of age who said he had been after the cows and did not know he had been shot at.

Taking up our return march we proceeded several miles and camped for the night making ourselves as comfortable as could be done under the circumstances, by setting brush and some old cornfodder up against the fence and crawling under it.

It got very cold in the night and snowed a little, and some of the boys found their hair frozen in the mud when they attempted to rise in the morning.

THEY WERE OURS BECAUSE WE NEEDED THEM.—After daylight some sheep and a hog or two were found. They were soon gobbled up and then gobbled down. We made coffee and after breakfast started on towards camp. The day became very hot and we had to march very slowly.

About two o'clock when still seven or eight miles from camp Captain Fisher was overcome with the heat. He was placed on one of the caissons until we reached a comfortable house, into which he was taken and kindly cared for by the lady of the house who said her husband was a major in the rebel army. After a few hours he was able to be brought into camp.

The command proceeded and reached camp about five o'clock P. M., June 6th very tired after their tramp of fifty-six miles.

Some of the boys threw themselves on the ground as soon as we got inside of the picket lines and after a rest came straggling in.

A courier had been sent to Lieutenant Parsons with orders to return with his command to camp, also, and he arrived about the same time.

When the detachments reached camp all was

bustle and activity as orders had been received for a move and it was said that we were to go to Washington City.

The past two days had been very dull ones for the boys who remained in camp as not enough were left for drill, and when the guards were sent out it seemed very lonesome to the handful remaining.

They had employed their time in washing and mending their clothes, and now looked so neat and clean, that the other boys said they were stuck up.

CASH ALL GONE.—The sutler at New Creek had done a pretty good business with the men, charging army prices, and by this time had got all their spare cash. A picture gallery had also been patronized and the tintypes sent home to the families and best girls, so they could see how we looked as real soldiers.

SOME VETERAN OFFICERS.—The post of New Creek was under command of a Mexican veteran Colonel Wilkinson. The—Illinois (the famous Col. Mulligans) which regiment having reenlisted was relieved by us to take the usual veteran furlough, had just gone and came back just after we left. Two officers of this regiment were left to assist Col. Wilkinson.

The Post Adjutant is a Captain Brown who is very irritable and at guard mounting, curses the men and flourishes his sword before them in a threatening manner when they do not march just to suit him.

His uniform consists of black broadcloth pants, a green woolen shirt and an ordinary fatigue cap.

The Sergeant Major is a stout built, swarthy looking, swaggering fellow who is said to be part Indian. His uniform is light gray pants, dark gray jacket, army shirt and slouch hat, with his pants in his boots.

The 133d so far has been quite actively engaged in Uncle Sam's work, not fighting to be sure, but in guarding stores, picketing the approaches to this important military depot, carrying supplies to the garrisons of different posts near here, and like work.

The men have done their duty in a soldierly manner, and will be ready for any work they may be called upon to perform.

CHAPTER VII.

ON TO WASHINGTON.—We at once got our traps ready, rations cooked, and at five o'clock P. M. June 7th took the cars for Washington city.

Just before sunset we reached Cumberland, Md., and were greeted by a large gathering of people who seemed quite patriotic, cheering, waving flags and handkerchiefs etc.

Through the night we went very slowly making only about forty miles. Sleeping in the cars packed like sardines was not very conducive to perfect rest, and the boys were glad to get out in the morning and cook their breakfast and stretch themselves.

At one of our stops there was a small store, and as usual the boys made a rush to purchase such articles as they needed.

The proprietor was overwhelmed with business and could not wait on his customers fast enough, so they began to help themselves, even those who had no money followed suit, and soon everyone had what he could lay hands on. On their return to the train they compared notes to see what each had secured. One fellow seemed to have been unsuccessful and was twitted by his comrades for his bad luck. He stood their jeers for a while, but finally pulled from under his coat a bottle of peppersauce saying, "By George! I did get something!" He was greeted by yells of Peppersauce! Peppersauce!

He always thereafter went by the name of Peppersauce, and when at roll call the orderly sergeant yelled out Peppersauce! he answered as promptly as if his proper name had been called. We then got aboard the cars again and slowly wended our way along toward Washington. The country is beautiful along the railroad, being mountainous country with rich valleys betwen the hills.

REBEL WORK.—When we reached Harpers Ferry we again saw the effects of war in the shape of burned shops and buildings, and wrecked cars.

Three locomotives and a good many cars had been run off the track on the Harpers Ferry side of the Potomac and dumped off the abutment into the river.

FINE SCENERY.—The view of the Potomac river here is fine. It is very wide and shallow with rocks peeping above the water, the swift current breaking over them and the reflection of the hills in the smooth places, altogether make a pretty scene. On the left are Maryland Heights where Ford surrendered to Stonewall Jackson. At six o'clock in the morning we passed Relay House and ran on to Annapolis Junction. Here we laid sidetracked for passing trains till dark. This gave us an opportunity to build fires and make coffee, which we were not slow to improve. Again boarding our palace cars, we composed ourselves in our berths (on the floor) and about two o'clock in the morning found ourselves in Washington.

We remained in the cars till five o'clock when we were quartered at the Soldier's Home.

While we were on the way here yesterday the National Republican convention at Baltimore renominated Abraham Lincoln for President and placed Andrew Johnson of Tennessee on the ticket with him for Vice President.

On arriving at Washington our Colonel reported to General Augur and was ordered to immediately put his command in light marching order, so that no man should have more than fourteen pounds to carry, then proceed to the Potomac river at the foot of Sixth Street, there take shipping and proceed to the White House on the Pamunkey river in Virginia and report to General Abercrombie to be sent to the Army of the Potomac. This order caused some fluttering of hearts and the boys who had originally expected to do home guard duty only, wondered how they could be taken right into the thick of the fray, for the Army of the Potomac had been for weeks fighting the battles of the Wilderness etc., and were still at it.

WE WERE NOT MUCH SCARED.—This feeling of trepidation was soon gone and when the order to fall in was given, every man took his place willingly and most of them cheerfuly although they had every reason to believe that the majority of them would leave their bones on the sacred soil of Old Virginia.

While in Washington the boys took advantage of their spare time to look about the Capitol and other buildings and enjoyed it very much, for few of them had ever seen the seat of the national government.

OHIO WAS THERE.—The people of Washington were amazed at the numbers of soldiers coming from Ohio, and when one told that *we* were from Ohio, exclaimed: "Great God! man! What kind of a damned machine have you got out there to make soldiers with?"

WHAT WE MAY GET. MAYBE!—The regiment marched without delay to the landing. Here we received another reminder of what might be our fate, boats we expected to take had just arrived loaded with wounded soldiers from the Army of the Potomac where we were going.

Their wounds were of every conceivable description. We were directed to assist in placing them in ambulances which were to take them to the hospitals, and did this service before we could embark.

While at the landing waiting to go on board, the peddlers of pies, fruits etc., came about very thick. The boys had very little money to buy with, but most of them tasted the wares. Several would gather round the vender and one in front would make a feint to help himself. This would cause the basket to be jerked back when it came into position for those in the rear to help themselves, which they did very liberally. The stock was soon disposed of but not to the profit of the dealers.

NOW FOR REAL WAR.—We boarded the Wenonah at three o'clock P. M. on June 10th, steamed down the river to Alexandria, coaled up and anchored for the night. It was an amusing sight for us northerners to see the darkies wheeling the coal onto the steamboat.

They had a regular time to go by and when a

certain place in the song was reached each man would grasp the handles of his wheelbarrow, fall in line with the rest, and step off to the music. There were twenty or thirty thus coming and going and the coal was soon loaded. The steamer was a good sized boat, but our regiment and the necessary baggage and supplies crowded it a good deal. As we came down the river we had a very good view of the forts and batteries, with their cannon pointing toward us, and we realized how quickly our steamboat could be sunk by them, had we not worn the blue.

We got no dinner and only hardtack for supper, but after the feast of oranges, pies, cakes, etc., before boarding the steamer we could stand it very well.

The decks were very dirty but tired soldiers can sleep anywhere so the night was passed quite comfortably. It was much better than being jolted in cattle cars. The weather was quite warm, but a good rain in the night cooled the air off nicely, and in the morning it got quite cold and drizzly with a strong wind blowing from the southwest.

TRIBUTE TO THE SEA.—A little after noon we got out into the Chesapeake bay and here the wind caused the waves to roll up pretty well, forming whitecaps as far as we could see. The result was that the rocking of the boat made many of the men seasick. They had quite a time "heaving Jonah" over the sides of the vessel and feeding the porpoises as the rest told them, and this was *worse* than cattle cars. The porpoises came rolling and tumbling about the boat in great numbers all the way down the bay and up the James River.

SEALED ORDERS.—Just before we started from Washington the Colonel had a large envelope handed him by an aide from General Augur's staff, endorsed "Not to be opened till in the Chesapeake bay." It proved to be an order changing our destination from White House to Bermuda Hundred where Butler had lately established himself with the Army of the James. During the progress down the bay we were out of sight of land a part of the time. We met several boats going up the bay carrying soldiers and wounded men to Washington. We passed Fortress Monroe about ten o'clock P. M. and anchored at Newport News for the night. Sunday morning June 12th we started on up the James which is very wide with low banks and level land beyond them until we got some distance up. Old Jamestown, the first settlement in Virginia, seemed ruined and deserted as did most of the towns we saw. This river is the main thoroughfare to the seat of war and consequently we were continually meeting ships and boats of all descriptions coming and going with their freight of soldiers or provisions and munitions of war. Here and there would be a gunboat patrolling the river, guarding us from rebel attacks, and one ironclad was passed, which sat low in the water and did not look to be of much consequence but if we could have seen the inside of her, it would have shown a wonder of equipments and men that would have dealt out destruction to the enemy on the shortest notice.

The plot keeps thickening and we are getting very near the point where real war exists. We will soon be with the veterans who have been in constant contact with the rebs for months.

CHAPTER VIII.

WE ARE AT THE FRONT.—About two o'clock P. M. we landed at Bermuda Hundred without any mishap, and on reporting to General Butler were ordered to Point of Rocks about four miles up the Appomattox. We arrived there about five o'clock and while waiting to be assigned our place in the works, took notice of what was passing around us.

Our men had built a lookout near where we stopped and the rebels had fired at it so much that it had to be abandoned, and they were still firing an occasional shot at it. Captain Steely went up to take a look at the structure which was built of pine poles after the fashion of a windmill frame. There was the report of a cannon from the rebel works and a conical shell struck the ground some distance in front of the captain and came tumbling end over end in his direction, throwing a shower of sand over him. He did not wait for it to come up with him but turned and made tracks away from it at a 2:40 gait calling forth cheers from the boys commending his agility. We pitched our tents in a woods close by and ate supper.

Our regiment was assigned to the First Brigade, First Division. Tenth Army Corps. Our brigade commander was General A. H. Terry who just then was promoted to division and then to Corps commander. Colonel Joshua B. Howell of the 85th

Penn. Vols. took command of the brigade, and General R. S. Foster of the division.

In our brigade was the Sixty-Seventh O. V. I. commanded by Colonel A. C. Voris now of Akron, O. To the officers and men of this veteran regiment the 133d was placed under obligations by many acts of kindness.

STATIONED ON THE LINE.—Monday June 13th. After breakfast we marched about a mile and a half from our camp to a point along the works about half way between the James and Appomattox.

Here we pitched our tents back some distance from the breastworks and cleared the ground of brush and fallen trees by piling it up and burning it. Every little while there would come a report from one of the burning brushheaps and there would be a scattering of the brands. This was caused by the unexploded bombshells which the rebels had thrown over at our men. The fires heated them enough to cause them to explode, but luckily no one was hurt by the flying pieces, though several had narrow escapes.

WE BUILD BOMB PROOFS.—As soon as we were settled here we were directed to build bomb proofs. This was done by building up poles four feet high, and then placing a roof of poles sloping up from them for ten or twelve feet. Then inside of this the ground was dug out a couple of feet deep also from around the shed and the earth thrown back of, and on top of the poles, thus making a sort of earth covered shed with the open side away from the enemy. Being covered with three feet or more of earth they were tolerably secure for us when firing took place from the rebel batteries.

The bomb proof of each company was about fifty feet long and ten feet or so wide with a six foot space between companies.

We were so diligent in getting them done that the old veterans laughed at us, saying that the old soldiers would have been three times as long about it. One reason for the work being done so soon was that the shells and cannon balls were alighting all about, which was quite a stimulant to exertion. Another was that most of our men were farmers inured to hard work and accustomed to driving their own business and they took hold of this in the same way. Two of our companies were city men not used to the shovel and spade so when they fell behind the others turned in and helped them.

Our fortifications here extend from the James to the Appomattox across the neck of a peninsula made by the junction of the two rivers and which comprises about thirty square miles of high and dry, healthy land which seems to be almost clear sand, and yet the cleared places are covered with corn which looks well.

Our troops have only been here about four weeks and the crops were planted before we came. It is a mystery to us northern men who have been used to rich land how anything grows on this sand.

A STRONG LINE.—Our line of fortifications here is very strong. At the banks of both rivers, there are bluffs about one hundred and twenty feet high. A deep and impassable ravine runs for half a mile from the James and one of the same kind for nearly a mile from the Appomattox across the neck of the peninsula toward each other, so that only a mile or so of strong works remained to be built. This rendered the line almost impregnable. The rivers were both deep up to the line of works, so that our gunboats could protect the peninsula and it was thus a splendid place to gather an army and to operate from, as troops and supplies could be brought by water very cheaply and quickly, and being close to both Richmond and Petersburg it was a valuable point to hold.

The rebel works are full of men in plain view about half a mile or less in front of us and their pickets and ours are close together. We got our bomb proofs completed but only occupied them about three hours when we were ordered to the breastworks to help repel an expected attack by Beauregard on Butler's center.

IN THE TRENCHES.—Their attack was a little slow, and a couple of brigades from our side sallied out and took a rebel redoubt with small loss. We laid in the trenches all night. On the morning of the fourteenth all the men able for duty, about eight hundred, were detailed to work on the fortifications and after marching to several places were finally put to work and made a road for Gen. A. J. Smith's corps of General Grant's army to pass over. We again laid all night in the trenches. The nights are uncomfortably cold while the days are very hot. On the fifteenth we could hear heavy firing all day in the direction of Petersburg. Troops are pouring in by the thousands and our position is constantly becoming stronger.

CHAPTER IX.

WE FIGHT FOR THE UNION. RAID ON THE RAILROAD.—On the morning of the sixteenth, after another night in the trenches we got our breakfast and were notified that all men able for work were detailed for fatigue duty in repairing, strengthening and extending breastworks around Bermuda Hundred. The detail was made, the men placed in line and had shouldered muskets, picks and shovels, when another order came directing the commandant to march to the front with every available man in his command with not less than forty rounds of amunition and two days rations per man, prepared to support a battery of artillery.

The reason for this move will be seen in the following dispatch.

HEADQUARTERS NEAR POINT OF ROCKS, VA.,
June 16, 1864—7:45 A. M.

Lieutenant-General U. S. Grant, Commanding Armies of the United States, City Point, Va.:

The enemy have evacuated our front. I have ordered out Foster's division to make a reconnoissance. The enemy have all gone to Petersburg. Hoke's division has come from the Army of Northern Virginia and gone to Petersburg. Will try to reach the railroad.

B. F. BUTLER,
Major-General Commanding.

TEARING UP THE RAILROAD.—We were ready at once and marching outside of our works and on through those of the rebs we formed a line of battle and advanced for a mile or more. The advance portion of our line reached the Richmond and Petersburg railroad, tore it up for some distance and burned the ties and bent the rails, as per the following report to General Grant:

JUNE 16, 1864—12:50 P. M.

Lieutenant-General Grant:

General Turner is now at Port Walthal Junction with 530 men, all the tried soldiers he has, tearing up the Petersburg railroad. General Terry has moved out on the turnpike and is endeavoring to strike the railroad there. I have ordered Kautz's cavalry in as I am very much in need of them to feel the enemy on the right.

B. F. BUTLER,
Major-General.

GENERAL BUTLER TO GENERAL TERRY,
HEADQUATERS DEPT OF VIRGINIA AND NORTH CAROLINA,
IN THE FIELD June 16, 1864.

General Terry:

Turner is now on railroad at junction tearing it up with about 500 men. General Butler suggests that you look well to your right and send part of your men to support of Turner, as the road well destroyed at one place is better than to poorly destroy it at several places. By this course you can cover your right and effectually destroy the road near where Turner now is. Make complete work of it. So far you have done splendidly.

The general has just notified General Grant that your forces are on the road.

Respectfully,

J. W. SHAFFER,
Colonel and Chief of Staff.

JUNE 16, 1864—2 P. M.

Col. J. W. Shaffer, Chief of Staff:

Ames and Foster both reached the turnpike. Foster near the junction of the Chester road. Ames at a point some distance to the south. Foster immediately became engaged with the enemy and a sharp skirmish ensued. It soon became apparent to him that the enemy were in force. I therefore halted Ames at the turnpike, but after a while directed him to send forward a picked party of men to tear up the railroad. Shortly after this order was given General Foster became so warmly engaged that I deemed it necessary to countermand it and withdraw General Ames' force to a position to cover Foster in case of need and to withdraw his own troops for a short distance. Prisoners taken say that the force in our front is Pickett's division, that it with other troops crossed the river this morning. They say they saw Lee in person at the crossing.

They also report that other troops, Lee's whole army are following Pickett.

Very respectfully your obedient servant,

ALF. H. TERRY,
Brigadier General.

June 16, 1864—3:15 p. m.

General Terry :

Dispatch received. You must withdraw as quickly and speedily as possible. I have sent word to Turner to withdraw also. You had better send an aide to him, so to do, also. See that your working parties are drawn in with their tools.

Benjamin F. Butler,
Major General Commanding.

LOOK! THEY'RE GOING TO CHARGE.—In withdrawing our brigade was assigned to the place of rear guard. The rebels advanced rapidly three lines deep and crowded us.

Colonel Howell commanding the brigade ordered us to about face and give them the warmest reception we could. He sent for Colonel Innis and handing him his field glass, said, "Look at those devils over there. They are going to charge on us." On looking through the glass Colonel Innis could distinctly see the Johnnies forming line of battle. Colonel Howell said, "Now, Colonel Innis, do not let them catch you without fixed bayonets."

"When shall I fix bayonets?" Colonel Innis asked. "Take your own time, only do not be caught with them unfixed."

WE GIVE THEM OUR BEST.—On came the rebs and about twenty-five rounds were exchanged with them about as rapidly as they could be fired. The effect of our fire on the enemy could not of course be told, but our brigade lost several men in killed and wounded, two of the latter being members of our regiment. In withdrawing our regiment was ordered to march by the right flank to close the line, which fortunately brought it back of the rebel works, and thus prevented our sustaining greater loss. The following order was issued to General Terry at this time:

GENERAL BUTLER'S HEADQUARTERS,
June 16, 1864—5:30 P. M.

General Terry :

Do not send off the Ohio Regiments ordered to Wilsons Wharf and Fort Powhatan until further orders.

B. F. BUTLER,
Major General.

(Copy to General Turner.)

Butler to Grant.]

JUNE 16, 1864—5:30 P. M.

Lieutenant-General Grant :

A GREAT BLUNDER.—Dispatch received. I have examined an intelligent deserter and prisoners. The evacuation was an enormous blunder.

Beauregard ordered out his troops and Longstreets Corps was to occupy their places, but Longstreet did not get up. I have improved the opportunity to destroy some three miles of the railroad. I will order my picket lines to hold, if possible, the line of the enemy's works, but as the line is so much longer than my old line I cannot hold it with my present force.

If we can hold on till Wright's two divisions come up we may then hold it.

Heavy skirmishing is now going on.

       B. F. BUTLER,
         Major General.

Butler to Terry.]

      JUNE 16, 1864—5:45 P. M.

General Terry:

Hold your picket line on the line of the enemy's works from Howlett's round to your front where our line was at first.

OUR DIVISION TO HOLD THE LINE.—Hold Ware Bottom Church with a strong reserve and do not yield without a struggle.

I hope to get up two divisions of Wright's Corps to occupy it during the night or early in the morning.

       BENJAMIN F. BUTLER.

Indorsement.

HEADQUARTERS TENTH ARMY CORPS,
  IN THE FIELD NEAR HATCHER'S RUN, VA.,
    June 16, 1864—6:25 P. M.

Brigadier General R. S. Foster, commanding First Division, is charged with the execution of this order.

By order of Brigadier-General Terry.

      ADRIAN TERRY,
    Captain and Assistant Adjutant-General.

JUST HOW IT WAS.—The following dispatch of General Butler to General Grant explains the entire situation.

JUNE 16, 1864—10:45 P. M.
Lieutenant-General Grant, Commanding, etc.:

The exact state of affairs in my front is this: At daybreak this morning the enemy's line was evacuated by the troops defending it, to go to Petersburg, from orders from Beauregard, but to leave a picket line which should amuse us till Early's Division should take their place. By a blunder the pickets were withdrawn on a part of the line. This was endeavored to be corrected about eight o'clock, but our pickets discovered the fact early in the morning and I ordered an advance along the whole line. This flanked the remaining pickets and all were driven in or captured. The railroad being thus opened we moved upon it at once and after throwing out a brigade toward our right to observe the enemy in the direction of Richmond, we commenced upon the railroad and have torn up the track for nearly three miles, piling up the ties, burning them with the rails laid over them, and in some places digging down the embankments. About 2 o'clock the enemy approached in force on our right and drove in our pickets, forcing us back to their line of intrenchments and near the James back to Ware Bottom Church. If we hold what we have now, we can turn their line at any time after Wright's Corps, which I have not yet heard of, comes up. I shall have three regiments on picket, after I withdraw five regiments, the whole eight being left out on that line to be sure to hold it, but as it leaves too large a force, being nearly one-half of my best men, to fight on a picket line and endangers the safety of my principal line, I withdraw the five regiments, especially as they have been working and fighting all day.

My right is within two miles of the turnpike, over which Lee must march as the railroad is gone, and within one mile of the gunboats. We are dropping shells up on it at intervals of once in three minutes, which is the firing you hear.

B. F. BUTLER,
Major General.

PRISONERS TAKEN. — Our brigade took about ninety or one hundred prisoners. Company "D" claimed the honor of capturing the first prisoner taken by the 133d, as a Johnny surrendered to privates John Q. Adams, Harrison Gilliland and John Wampler at about 10 o'clock A. M. The warm reception given the rebels prevented their following us farther and we arrived inside our works at 11 o'clock at night, having been under fire for about fifteen hours. Three companies on the left of the regiment, B., G. and K., were detached from the others when we went out and placed on the extreme left of the line, and did not participate in the engagement, but the skirmishers in front of them were continually engaged and the bullets and cannon balls flew over their heads thickly, and kept them anxiously waiting for the order to go in, for which they were quite ready.

A CLOSE CALL.—When the order was given to fall back, the regiment halted at the first convenient place to see that all were present. These companies being absent the Colonel asked some one to volunteer to carry an order to their captains to rejoin the regiment.

Private Joseph Gregg at once offered to perform the duty, and started to carry the order. On arriving at the breastworks, which the regiment had just left, the messenger seeing a lot of soldiers behind them ran up and said, "The Colonel directs that you join the regiment immediately." The reply was, "That is a Yankee, catch him." Gregg turned and ran for dear life and liberty, and some six or eight rebels ran to catch him, but he was too swift to be picked up, and with these men behind him the rebels could not fire on him for fear of killing their own men. They yelled to their men to fall to the ground, and give them a chance to shoot. This the pursuers soon did, and more than a hundred shots were aimed at Gregg. Three balls cut his hat, some five others cut his clothing, but not a drop of blood flowed. It was in consequence of this failure to have these companies rejoin the regiment that they missed the fun near Ware Bottom Church later in the afternoon, which they very much regretted.

PART RAN—BUT CAME BACK AGAIN.—During the hottest part of the engagement the Second Maine Infantry on the left of our brigade, finding their ammunition exhausted, made a movement to the rear for the purpose of filling up again. Seeing this, a good part of the 133d supposed an order had been given to retreat, and they became excited and went back in a hurry. They soon discovered their mistake, however, and re-formed their line on the double-quick, when the whole brigade cheered lustily and opened up a furious fire along the whole line. They exchanged some twenty-five rounds of musketry, when the enemy fell back leaving about ninety prisoners in our hands. During the balance of the engagement the 133d behaved like old veterans.

About a company and a half of the men did not run, and while General Howell was rallying the rest he ordered Colonel Innis to remain in front in charge of the line, which he did to the entire satisfaction of the brigade commander.

General Foster and staff assisted in restoring confidence in the men, and not finding the Colonel with them supposed he had abandoned his command, but his remaining at his post explains why he was not with the fugitives.

The following dispatches bearing on this subject will explain the matter.

GENERAL BUTLER'S HEADQUARTERS,
June 17, 1864—Received at 11:15 P. M.
General Terry:

It is reported that the Colonel of the Ohio regiment that broke and ran yesterday, ran away from his regiment. If so, please report facts, and if he ran and did not attempt to rally his men, he will be properly dealt with.

J. W. SHAFFER,
Colonel and Chief of Staff.

THE COLONEL STAYED.—
HEADQUARTERS TENTH ARMY CORPS,
June 17, 1864—4.30 P. M.
General Terry, at General Butler's Headquarters:

Colonel Howell reports that Colonel Innis when

his regiment broke, remained at the front with about half a company, which he kept up to the line, and that he deserves credit rather than blame.

A. TERRY,
Assistant Adjutant-General.

Colonel Howell, commanding our brigade, says in his report of the fight:

"About 4 or 5 o'clock I got the order to fall back, which was done in perfect coolness and order, no confusion, no hurry.

We fell back in the rifle pits on a line with Ware Bottom Church, the place designated. About sunset the enemy made a dash upon us. My old brigade held their ground nobly. The One Hundred and Thirty-third being new to fire broke and ran, with the exception of two or three companies. I respectfully beg leave here to state that the conduct of Colonel Innis was irreproachable.

I rode up and down the line and saw him cool and composed, and trying to rally his men. My horse was shot under me at this time. I wish to say to the general that these men are unused to fire, they have to be educated to it. My belief is that they will never break again. I believe they are brave men, they came back with a cheer, those that I saw."

JOSHUA B. HOWELL,
Colonel Eighty-fifth Pennsylvania Vols., Comm'd'g Brigade.

The rebels kept up their cannonading at intervals all night, as also did our artillery, while we maintained our position at the breastworks until one o'clock the next day, June 17th.

CHAPTER X.

WE GO TO ANOTHER POST.—We now left the front for Fort Powhatan, about twelve miles down the river, in obedience to the following order:

HEADQUARTERS TENTH ARMY CORPS,
IN THE FIELD, June 17, 1864.

SPECIAL ORDERS }
No. 53.   }

Pursuant to instructions from department headquarters the One Hundred and Thirty-third Ohio Volunteers will proceed at once to the commissary wharf at Point of Rocks and report to Major Haggerty for duty at Fort Powhatan, relieving the command of Colonel Stafford, which will return on the same boat to Point of Rocks.

Quartermasters will furnish transportation.
By order of Brigadier-General A. H. Terry.

ADRIAN TERRY,
Captain and Assistant Adjutant-General.

During the forenoon while we were lying at the breastworks, before receiving the above order, there was quite a skirmish in the woods in front of us, and our gunboats have been throwing shells occasionally all day. Just as we were about to leave, the Johnnies began to shell our camp, but did not harm us.

GENERAL BUTLER COMPLIMENTS US.—
At the landing where we were to take the boat we met several of the 5th U. S. C. T., some of whom are from Columbus.

While we were waiting to take the boat a staff officer rode up and inquired for Colonel Innis. Finding him he said, "Colonel, you are the hardest man to find there is in Bermuda Hundred." The Colonel explained how we had been ordered about on various duties and that we had been busy.

He then said, "General Butler sends his compliments to the 133d for the handsome manner in which they behaved after rallying from their break. He understands that they are new to fire and was pleased that they did so well."

Boarding the steamboat we were not long coming in sight of the fort, but instead of landing us the boat anchored for the night.

We had been in the trenches several nights and on fatigue duty in the daytime, then came the days marching and fighting, so that the men were very tired.

The boat's decks afforded a good place to lie down and there was no guard duty to perform, so as soon as we cast anchor and dusk came, every one laid down and put in a full night sleeping. This was the best night's rest we had had since we left home.

AN ARMY ON THE MOVE.—Just ahead of our boat is a pontoon bridge, on which a portion of Grant's forces, Meade's Army of the Potomac, is crossing the river, and above and below they are crossing by ferry boats.

They have been crossing without ceasing for three days and nights, which gives one some idea of the immense number of men there are. The immense lot of stores, ammunition, provisions, tents etc, and droves of cattle, numbering thousands, all go to make up the army.

AN AGREEABLE CHANGE.—Our regiment was quite well satisfied to change from active duty in the field to garrison duty in the fort. They thought it more in accordance with the orders under which they were called out. They did not think they had been sufficiently prepared for duty at the front, though the active drilling they had at New Creek made them better than many old regiments in the field.

On June 18th, as soon as it was light, our boat moved up to the wharf and we landed and marched up hill into the fort.

BUTLER'S IDEA OF THE PLACE.—In speaking of Fort Powhatan, General Butler says:

"It will be observed from the instructions which I gave General Hinks who commanded the troops holding Fort Powhatan, that I was exceedingly anxious for the safety of that point because that was the weak point of my whole position.

For although it was some twelve miles below City Point on the James, yet if it were once in possession of the enemy, it would be impossible to get any troops or supplies up the river, as the channel ran close under it. My experience with Vicksburg, which was on a bluff high above the possible range of the guns of the fleet, which were not mortar, told me that if Fort Powhatan were once captured by the rebels, it could be easily held against the naval vessels.

I was anxious lest it be taken by surprise, and therefore from day to day almost, I persisted in cautioning Major General Hinks, who was in command. It may be asked why, if it was of so much importance, I entrusted its defenses to a garrison of negro troops?

TO FIGHT DESPERATELY.— I knew that they would fight more desperately than any white troops in order to prevent capture, because they knew that if captured they would be returned into slavery under Davis' proclamation, and the officers commanding them might be murdered. So there was no danger of a surrender. The capture of Fort Powhatan or Fort Pocahontas or both by the rebels, would render it impossible for Grant to cross his army over the James."

The colored troops held the fort, and Grant's army was crossing when we got there. We relieved these colored troops who were expected to do such desperate fighting.

It can be seen by the foregoing account how important a duty we had to perform.

On arriving here Colonel Innis, being the ranking officer, assumed command of the post, and turned over the immediate command of the regiment to Lieutenant Colonel Ewing.

ALL KINDS OF SOLDIERS.—In the forces serving here every arm of the service is represented. Two naval officers in command of gunboats, one placed above, the other below the fort, a detachment of the Third Pennsylvania Heavy Artillery, under command of Captain Von Shilling, a squadron of cavalry, a detachment of the First New York Engineers, also a signal corps and telegraph station.

The 133d was now brigaded with the 138th, 143d and 163d regiments of Ohio Volunteers, and formed the 1st Brigade, 3d Division of the 10th Army Corps. Brigade Headquarters were at Fort Pocahontas (Wilson's Landing) under command of Brigadier General Gilman Marston.

While we were here our duties were various. For fatigue duty we completed the fort and fortifications around it in the most substantial manner.

A TROUBLESOME TASK.—Part of our work was to keep up twenty miles of telegraph line through a rebel country and connecting General Grant's headquarters with the government at Washington City.

The following dispatches will show some of the work done in this connection.

FORT POWHATAN, July 10, 1864.

Major General Butler:

I have had the telegraph wire repaired below here and I have got reason to believe that the inhabitants along the line protect and harbor the men that destroy it. My officer reports that they were fired upon three times from houses on Cabin Point. What course shall I pursue in regard to citizens along the line?

G. S. INNIS,
Colonel Commanding Post.

HEADQUARTERS U. S. FORCES,
FORT POWHATAN, VA., July 12, 1864.

Major General B. F. Butler, Commanding Department of Virginia and North Carolina, General:

Is it expected that I will give all the aid in my power to repair and keep up the U. S. military telegraph from this place to Swan Point in preference to working on the fortifications here?

Very respectfully,
G. S. INNIS,
Colonel Commanding Post.

GENERAL BUTLER'S HEADQUARTERS,
July 12, 1864.

Col. G. S. Innis:

You will do all you can to keep the telegraph in repair.

By command of Major General Butler.
R. S. DAVIS,
Assistant Adjutant-General.

FORT POWHATAN, July 21, 1864.

General Butler:

The telegraph wire is cut again between here and Swan Point, which occurs about every second or third day. Shall I hold the citizens along the line responsible that this is not repeated on fear of having their buildings destroyed near points where it is cut? Please answer.

G. S. INNIS,
Colonel Commanding Post.

Answer.

HEADQUARTERS DEP'T OF VA. AND NORTH CAROLINA,
July 21, 1864—8 P. M.

Colonel G. S. Innis:

Unless citizens give you information before the act who it is and where they are, that are engaged in cutting the telegraph, burn their buildings and catch and hold some of the principal ones as hostages to be hanged if the outrage is repeated.

BENJAMIN F. BUTLER,
Major General.

HOSTAGES TAKEN.—

HEADQUARTERS U. S. FORCES,
FORT POWHATAN, VA., July 23, 1864.

Major General Butler, Commanding Department of Vir- and North Carolina, General:

I have again repaired the U. S. Military telegraph line from this place to Swan Point.

I caused four citizens to be brought in as hostages, and had the people living along the line notified that they would be held responsible for the safety of that line. What shall I do with these hostages? Since they were brought in I have learned that one of them, a minister, relieved and dressed the wounds of one of our soldiers, cared for him till morning, then sent him to this fort.*

I am very respectfully your obedient servant,

G. S. INNIS,
Colonel Commanding Post.

*This is the minister referred to in Comrade Ender's account. His name was Murdock, and his wife claimed to belong to the Custis family, and that she was a great grand-daughter of Martha Washington.

The guard house was a crude affair, and was covered only with boughs, so that with the rain we had it was not a comfortable place to keep the prisoners in. The Colonel therefore asked if he could not send them to Bermuda Hundred — as per the following dispatch:

FORT POWHATAN, July 26, 1864.

Major General Butler:

I have arrested three prominent citizens between here and Swan point held as hostages for safety of telegraph line. I cannot well keep them here. Shall I send them to Bermuda Hundred?

G. S. INNIS,
Colonel Commanding.

Which General Butler indorsed thus:

Hold onto them, so as to execute them if necessary on the spot.

BENJAMIN F. BUTLER.

DESPAIR OF HOSTAGES.—When this indorsement was received Colonel Innis took it to the guard house and read it to the prisoners. The Rev. Murdock asked, "Did General Butler send such a dispatch as that?"

"He certainly did," was answered.

Then turning to his companions the minister said, "Brethren, give up all hope of life. We are as dead men."

The Colonel said, "I did not bring this to alarm you, but to save you. If you will write letters to your friends telling them the state of affairs and what General Butler has ordered, I will have them delivered by my cavalry." They at once fell to writing urgent letters to their families.

The minister's letter to his wife was very pathetic, and closed "with love to all our family, both white and black."

The letters were duly delivered and in a couple of days about three hundred women appeared at our picket line and desired to come into the fort to intercede for the preacher. They did not seem anxious about the others, but none were allowed to come in except Mrs. Murdock.

Another of the hostages was a Mr. Harrison, who owned a plantation near the fort. He was a relative of the rebel congressman, W. B. Harrison, whose plantation we visited, four miles down the river. He was greatly grieved over his arrest and shed tears, saying, "Only think, I have always been opposed to secession, and made twenty-three speeches against it before Virginia seceded, and now I am arrested by my own government."

His case was investigated and he was found loyal and at once released. He used frequently to come into the fort after that, and nearly always brought some delicacy to the officers, if nothing more than a piece of ice.

The effect of General Butler's order was very good, for we had no more trouble for a while. The hostages were paroled, as shown below.

HOSTAGES PAROLED.—

FORT POWHATAN, VA., July 27, 1864.
General B. F. Butler:

J. J. Deal, a prisoner here pledges his honor as

a man and by everything he holds sacred, should he be released, to do everything in his power to prevent the telegraph line from being cut. Should he fail in this he pledges himself to inform on and guide our troops to the hiding places of those that cut the wire. He also wishes to take the oath of allegiance, leave the State and remove to Cincinnati, Ohio, with his family. Had I better try him?

G. S. INNIS,
Colonel Commanding.

FORT POWHATAN, July 28, 1864.

Major General Butler:

I have yet in my custody two hostages. They both say they are anxious to take the oath of allegiance. They pledge themselves to do all in their power to prevent the telegraph wire from being cut. They further agree to become answerable with their lives for the faithful performance of their obligation. Shall I try them?

G. S. INNIS,
Colonel Commanding.

Answer.

HEADQUARTERS DEP'T VA. AND NORTH CAROLINA,
IN THE FIELD July 28, 1864.

Colonel Innis, Fort Powhatan:

Yes. Administer the oath to them all and try them. Both dispatches received.

BENJAMIN F. BUTLER,
Major General.

FORT POWHATAN, July 29, 1864.

General B. F. Butler, Commanding, General:

I believe I am in possession of reliable information as to the hiding place of the guerrillas who cut the wires between here and Swan Point. Can you send me three or four squadrons of cavalry to assist in capturing them?

G. S. INNIS,
Colonel Commanding.

HEADQUARTERS DEP'T OF VA. AND NORTH CAROLINA,
IN THE FIELD July 29, 1864—6:40 P. M.

Col. G. S. Innis, Port Powhatan:

Keep watch of the guerrillas. I will send you cavalry in a couple of days.

J. W. SHAFFER,
Colonel and Chief of Staff.

KILLED BY BUSHWHACKERS.—In spite of all our caution, several of our garrison were killed by concealed rebels, but fortunately none of them were members of the 133d.

CHAPTER XI.

EXCITING AND DANGEROUS SERVICE.—
The following sketch of this telegraph service is given by Comrade John C. Ender, now of Chicago, who was detailed to assist in the repairs.

He says: "This duty took me out on the road every morning with a squad of Company D., First U. S. Colored Cavalry, as the wires were cut every night after midnight. On our first trip we had only one wagon, which was drawn by a pair of old worn-out mules with a plow harness which had been in existence for many moons, and which consisted of bridle, collar, hames and traces, there being no back-straps, belly-bands or saddles. The command was in the habit of bringing in colored refugees. On this day a colored man joined the party with a view of bringing in his family and what furniture he could carry with the meagre outfit we had. We reached the spot where we found the wire cut, without any opposition, and repaired it. We expected to feed, allowing the man with the team to get his family a few miles beyond, when we were notified by a colored man that a party of rebel cavalry, several hundred strong, had just crossed a few miles away and were heading toward us. The captain said we must retrace our steps at once, advising me and Andy Renner of Company I., who was with us, to mount the mules, and should we be attacked to cut the hame straps and leave the wagon.

In this position we rode six or seven miles on lean mules, without saddle or blanket. We were well satisfied to know we were out of reach of the enemy. This made us apply to our worthy quartermaster Bancroft for horses, of which several stray ones had been brought in from the surrounding country.

The regiment will all remember our return daily from these trips as we invariably got in when the regiment was on dress parade outside of the fort, and always got a cheer when we showed a good supply of forage, of which the old carriage was always well filled. After getting a mount, my duty called me to City Point. The telegraph wire between City Point and Fort Powhatan was in less danger than between Powhatan and Swan Point. We considered it safe to go alone or in pairs to City Point. I always went as an escort. We were always on the lookout for a surprise.

HALT.—On one occasion, when about seven or eight miles out from City Point, we met three Confederate cavalry coming down a crossroad. We got out on the road too far and saw we were noted. Knowing our nearest shelter was the outpost of City Point, we headed in that direction. Having miscalculated our distance, we ran on our vidette post before we saw him, as the sun was shining very bright in our faces, and the cavalry picket was under the shade of a small tree. We heard the word "Halt!" and looking in the direction of the voice we saw the bright barrel of his carbine pointing directly at me. To check up and dismount was but one movement.

When we approached and explained our haste, the soldier with pale face and excitement said he had seen the same three rebs only an hour before reconnoitering, and thought they dared to charge him, and only for our blue uniforms, which he noticed as we approached, he would have pulled the trigger. We were thankful for his good judgment, and only after a long rest and with many good wishes did we continue our journey.

Our quarters at City Point were at General Grant's headquarters at the White House on the point of the river. It was there I traded the gray mare which had been picked up outside of Powhatan, having been run down and turned loose as being unfit for any further use. She had picked up considerably and was in fair condition. The roan horse I traded her for gave entire satisfaction to our quartermaster, being in much better condition. I learned afterward that the gray mare was shipped to Washington. Not having been branded she was private property, and being quite a fleet animal, she won in several races. The roan horse was kept at Powhatan.

I had many a pleasant trip to City Point with hardly enough incidents to mention here. A case of endurance came before my notice while with the telegraph corps at Powhatan.

PITIFUL CASE.—On one of our trips out to repair the wire we met the old minister of Cabin Point (whose name I have forgotten), about seven miles out, with a wornout cavalry horse, a rope harness, and a home-made two-wheeled cart. Upon it he was bringing a wounded Union soldier who had reached his house the evening before in a nearly exhausted condition. I was detailed to return with them to Powhatan. On the way back the man gave me the history of his sad experience and how he was wounded. He belonged to an Eastern regiment which was just returning with Wilson's command from what was known as Wilson's Raid.

Many of the horses besides his comrades' and his own gave out on the retreat, and in order to keep up with the command they abandoned their horses and set out across the country. Three of the men got cut off from the rest and were captured by bushwhackers, who pressed them back out of sight of the command, expecting, as they said, to capture more. Towards evening they gave it up and while going through the woods, they, without a moments' notice, shot the three prisoners. The next morning this man revived, having been shot five times. His two comrades were dead. He remembered crossing a small stream just before the firing commenced. Wending his way back as best he could, he reached the creek and threw himself into it, which made him feel quite refreshed. While he lay on the bank drying himself he knew not what his fate would be, when, as if by magic, there came a wornout government horse (the one hitched to the cart) which had strayed to the creek looking for water.

The animal noticing the blue uniform, came at his call, and with great effort he mounted it thinking it might get him out of the woods. They wandered about till dark, when the man spied a light ahead.

Guiding his horse in the direction of the light brought him out on the road and to the house of the minister of Cabin Point.

The presence of the soldier made the minister uneasy, as the rebel scouts, bushwhackers and regular cavalry were on the lookout in the neighborhood at all times, and to find him harboring a Union soldier would be resented by revenge. However, as the poor fellow could go no further, he was obliged to shelter him. Placing the wounded man on the rear porch, he rigged up the cart outfit and started with him towards Powhatan, in which condition we met them on our trip out. We placed him in the hospital at the Fort, where our surgeon examined him and gave very little hope for his recovery. In a few days he was sent by boat to Washington, where we lost trace of him. After twenty-two years I read an account in an eastern paper, giving the dates and locations as I have stated them, saying the man was still alive, but never had been able to walk again, one side being paralyzed from the wounds.

He was applying for an increase of pension. I forwarded the clipping to Mr. Phillip Bruck, of Columbus, who was our Hospital Steward at Fort Powhatan, who wrote me that he remembered the man and the circumstance quite well. I lost the man's address and so never had an opportunity of getting any further information regarding this wonderful case.

A RUN FOR LIFE.—One of my never-to-be-forgotten adventures while serving with the telegraph corps happened shortly before we left Fort Powhatan.

The rebels got bolder every day, as they found our force was quite small. Our Colonel no doubt remembers the incident, as thereafter a large force accompanied the repair men. The old saying, "What is one man's loss is another man's gain", came true on the trip out in question. On the day previous, the 1st Lieutenant of Company D., 1st U. S. Colored Cavalry, was thrown from his horse, which was a very vicious animal, and got badly hurt. That evening I got him to consent to let me ride the animal out the next day. We started about daybreak in the morning, got beyond Brandon Mills and found the wire cut. In testing between us and Swan Point we found the circuit also broken. We spliced the wire and started to find the next break, which we did at a place called Spring Grove, about eleven miles out. There the wire ran across lots to the next crossroad. The old man upon whose plantation the wire was cut, told us that some 300 southern cavalry had just gone by and cut the wire. We tested and found all right, but a break between us and Fort Powhatan, which had been made since we left a few hours before. The Lieutenant said, "This means trouble." We were only about fifty men. One white officer, 2nd Lieutenant of Company D., 1st U. S. Colored Cavalry, the man who repaired the wire, and myself with testing battery. The balance were all colored troops. We repaired the wire in the field and notified the man of the place.

General Butler had given strict orders to arrest any person upon whose place the wire was found cut.

With the explanation he gave us, we concluded

to report our finding and arrest him later if the
authorities thought proper. Making our way back
to find the new break, we met a colored woman who
told us her boy had just come from near Brandon
Mills and had met a large body of southern cavalry.
They had taken down a large stretch of wire, where
the line runs through the woods, had placed trip-
wires across the road, and a fence of rails back of
it. The Lieutenant said, "They have laid a trap.
The party who cut the wire through the field is not
the same which is between us and Powhatan. Their
game is to start us toward the trap and massacre
the whole outfit, as they are bitter against white officers of colored troops and never give the colored
troops any quarter. We have no time for planning.
To go to the river means to get caught. If we go
farther into the country we are liable to meet larger
forces, as scouts from Petersburg are always out
there. We have only one remedy—to cut our way
through. I will take four men for advance guard,
go to the trap, take up the wire and take down the
fence. They will not be likely to fire on so small a
force. At the first fire you must all come forward
on a charge." As the Lieutenant afterwards explained, there was no firing until they had several
rails off the fence. His horse cleared the obstruc-
tion, when from the woods near by voices hallooed.
By this time the advance had the wire loose and quite
a gap in the fence, when a continuous firing commenced. The vicious horse I had did me good service, clearing the gap without a break. The whole
command scattered along by ones and twos. There

were two killed and several wounded. Some had their horses shot and did not get to the fort for several days. As we left there shortly afterwards I never heard a full report of the engagement."

SHAMEFUL OUTRAGE.—The two mentioned by Comrade Ender as being killed were colored cavalrymen.

The rebels stripped their bodies of clothing, mutilated them shamefully and left them in the public road. This action of the rebs called for revenge, and it was partly for this purpose that the expedition spoken of below by Comrade Westervelt was sent out.

CHAPTER XII.

A THRILLING EXPERIENCE. — Comrade (now the Rev.) H. B. Westervelt gives the following account of an "outing" of his in connection with the telegraph.

"The special service required of us was to keep the river open and to protect the telegraph line.

This, by the way, was the great problem. A telegraph line runs out into the country, across streams, over bogs, through forests, along miles and miles of lonely roadway. An army might not get there, but a few men could work through, and covered by the dense underbrush which filled those pine forests, could go where they wished, and be completely concealed at almost any point. As would be expected, the wires were cut very frequently.

The line men were kept busy. Scouting parties were frequently sent out. A few prisoners were brought in, but the nuisance was unabated. Often before the scouts or repairers got in, the wires would be broken again. This state of affairs gave rise to the incident I am asked to relate.

On Monday, August 1st, I came off picket duty and was allowed to rest during most of the day. In the evening, about the time we were spreading our blankets, some one called my name. I went out and was taken a little ways from the tent and the case was laid before me.

The interruption of communications through the cutting of the wires was becoming very annoying, indeed almost unbearable. Our present methods were thoroughly inadequate. The enemy could dodge us every time and slip up and cut the wires even before the retiring scouts were out of hearing. The only way to stop it would be to go out and lie for them, watch the wires and be on hand to intercept the mischief. Lieutenant Darrah (of Company A.) had volunteered to lead a party of this kind, and he wanted only men who had seen previous service. Would I be one of them?

It can be seen that a service of this kind was not particularly desirable. "Lying in the brush" did not count for much, but the service asked was one of peculiar and extreme peril. Our neighbors, across the line did not hesitate to conceal themselves and shoot down our troops, but they were greatly horrified if we should undertake it, and parties wearing the blue and doing that kind of thing, would, probably, if captured, be hung to the nearest tree.

I remember while we were talking our Colonel with whom I was well acquainted, rode up and insisted that there was no compulsion toward such a service, and rather dissuaded me from going. I told the messenger that if Lieutenant Darrah was going and wanted me, I would be one of his squad.

I returned to my tent, got my accoutrements, and was away. It was held necessary to keep the matter an entire secret, so I said nothing to my tentmates, except that I was on duty. We were gone nearly thirty-six hours and when we returned my comrades merely supposed I was on an extended term as picket somewhere.

A NIGHT TRIP.—We left camp about one o'clock in the night or early morning of the 2d. We marched to Brandon Church, an abandoned Episcopal church about five miles out, then quietly worked our way out along the line to a crossroad some three-quarters of a mile further on, reaching there just as day was breaking. Here we concealed ourselves in the brush. There was a house just across the road, and not more than six or eight rods from where we were concealed. We could hear the humming of the spinning wheel all day. In the morning the children came out in the road and seeing our footprints in the dust, wondered how so many footmarks got there. We, not more than fifty feet off, almost held our breath till they went away. We lay there all day and not an inmate of that house had the least idea that a soldier was nearer than the fort. At night guards were told off, and the rest lay down to sleep. But now another problem presented itself. We had left the fort hurriedly and with the greatest secrecy. Hence provisions were running low, indeed they were scarce when we started. We had no wish to return without accomplishing something, so a couple started out to find a colored family whom they knew, to get corn pone for the crowd. There were thirteen of us. At eleven o'clock I went on guard. I was ordered to be very careful until our foragers came in, after which I was to challenge no one, but shoot at any one who should come along. Soon our boys came in with the word that they had been successful, but would have to return about two o'clock, as the "Auntie" would have to bake the pone. It was raining a little and was very dark. The company was all asleep but the Corporal (Joe Gregg, my tentmate, now Department Commander of the G. A. R. of Montana) lay by my side telling me to wake him if I heard anything, or at the expiration of my time.

A CRITICAL MOMENT.—Between twelve and one o'clock I heard the sound of horses approaching from the direction of the church and fort.

I pushed Joe and we were ready. Two men came on horses to the crossroads where we were lying, and turned off the telegraph road into the one running west. They checked up at once and one said, "I guess there are no scouts out to-night" (Joe declared "he said Yankee scouts", but I did not catch that). "No, it is a bully night for us!" They now turned back upon the telegraph road and Joe fired. One man threw up his hands and cried out, "Oh! my God! I'm shot! I'm killed!" The other spurred up and caught and held him on his horse, crying out, "For God's sake, men, don't shoot! You are firing on your own men." During this time I held my fire. It is a serious thing to shoot a man, and if that man was one of us it would be calamitous. "Friends to whom?" shouted our lieutenant. "Friends to the Southern flag." Then I fired, but the horses were plunging, they were further off, and the aim was not true. The horses galloped back toward the church, and we gathered up our traps and got ready for action.

OUR ESCAPE.—The lieutenant decided that as

we were now located, our position was perilous, and we had better move. It would not do to start directly for the fort. The horsemen had gone that way and we would probably meet a force too strong for us.

In the pine woods of the South there are few fences, and the roads or driveways are numerous. This was fortunate for us.

We struck out eastwardly from our ambush. As we went out that road the enemy returned along the telegraph line toward the point of ambush. About a mile east we struck another road running west toward the church and fort. We turned into this, the enemy following on the road east. It will thus be seen that as we passed along one side of the triangle, they followed us on another.

We finally reached the church and as it adjoined a swamp we concluded to lie there until daylight. There were woods all around us. We lay close to, and east of the church in some tall grass and under the boughs of a tree. The enemy had probably some thirty or forty men, but in the darkness they had no way of learning our strength nor exact position, without more risk than they cared to assume.

We heard them on three sides of us at once as they reconnoitered, but after an hour or so everything grew still.

TICKLISH RECONNOITERING.—Before long the lieutenant, hopeful and yet suspicious, ordered me to cross the open space north to a ravine running out from the swamp to see whether I could find anything. He had probably forgotten that my turn as guard had expired. Now I never was inclined to boast of courage when in the face of danger, but this time I am frank to confess I was afraid. In crossing that space of perhaps one hundred yards I did not take one step. That was the only time in my life that I emulated a snake and sighed for greater thinness. Bless the man that invented tall grass! I made the trip, investigated among the trees, satisfied myself that the enemy had disappeared, and then lest I might become satisfied that he had returned I got down and crawled back utterly oblivious of the fact that it had rained and that tall grass when wet, does not add to one's appearance.

We lay there till towards day, then shifted our position and in the morning marched back to the fort. Parties coming in during the day brought word that the man shot had died and his body had been left in the old mill.

RATHER DO SOMETHING ELSE.—One well grounded preference was stamped on my mind. I had been under fire, been in battle, gone on scouts, and I would rather do them all (at once if possible) than to play bushwhacker. It is not pleasant in itself, and the outlook if captured is miserable.

One thing more I am sure of: Soldiers can if necessary be quiet. For nearly thirty-six hours our band did not speak above a whisper.

One other reminiscence is in place. We missed our corn-pone. It never hunted us up, and we charged it to profit and loss."

TERRIBLE PUNISHMENT.—The rebels soon organized another force for the purpose of cutting the wire and doing us such other harm as they could! It consisted of ten men under a Captain Ruffin who was a native of the neighborhood.

Colonel Innis was soon informed of this fact and of their movements by the man who brought honey, butter, eggs, etc., to the fort for sale to the officers. He was a half simple looking fellow who was not considered fit for service in the rebel army, and so was allowed to remain at home, but he proved a keen observer of operations in his vicinity and brought valuable information to the commandant at the fort. The Colonel learned that this band was in the habit of taking supper at midnight at a certain house, as did the other band. He telegraphed to General Butler asking for one hundred cavalry, saying he thought a good service could be done by them. The dispatch was sent in the morning and along toward evening a couple of boats were seen coming down the river full of men and horses. Arriving opposite the fort they rounded to and landed a hundred cavalry under command of Major Hamilton who said he was a grandson of Alexander Hamilton of revolutionary fame. Colonel Innis gave him a map of the locality to be visited and told him he wished to hear that in the morning he had eleven prisoners or that there were eleven new graves at Brandon Mills. Next morning as the colonel was dressing, Major Hamilton's adjutant appeared and said, "Colonel Innis, the Major sends his compliments and reports that there are eleven new graves at Brandon Mills."

The adjutant gave the details of the affair. The rebels entered the house designated and were at supper when our force surrounded the place. A sergeant with a dozen men was sent to demand their surrender. Opening the door he marched his men in and made his demand. Instead of surrendering they endeavored to escape by the windows and were sabred by the troops outside, not a shot being fired.

CHAPTER XIII.

GREAT RESPONSIBILITY.—Our most important duty was to guard the James, so as to allow the passage of vessels back and forth with troops and supplies and wounded and prisoners. The river being the main thoroughfare to the seat of war it was very necessary to keep it open. There was hardly any time that boats could not be seen going and coming. Sometimes as many as thirty were in sight at once.

When the rebels were firing on our transports, the passing boats hove to under the guns of the fort, till there was quite a fleet of them, passing on as soon as the danger was over.

Some of the vessels conveying prisoners were fairly swarming with Johnnies in their butternut suits. They seemed to take their captivity very cheerfully, and when we would cheer at their passing they would yell lustily in return.

One thing that bore evidence of the destruction that war causes, was the number of dead mules that floated down the river.

It was a common occurrence for the enemy to attack our shipping loaded with supplies for the army investing Petersburg and Richmond.

The guns of Fort Powhatan were turned upon these raiders, and in no instance was the foe successful in capturing a boat or the least article on its way for the convenience or subsistence of our comrades at the front.

BE VIGILANT.—Frequently while at this fort, the commandant would receive a note of warning from General Grant's headquarters informing him of the importance of being vigilant in the discharge of his duty as to watchfulness, and being at all times fully prepared to repel an attack from the enemy, and these notes wound up generally by saying, "The safety of this whole army depends largely on your vigilance at Fort Powhatan."

DID NOT WANT TO GO.—Lieutenant Baldwin, the engineer officer in charge, was afraid he would be sent to the front and therefore delayed the finishing of Fort Powhatan all he dared. He made considerable complaint about not being furnished with men for the work. He also was a pretty hard drinker, which interfered with his usefulness.

The following are some of the dispatches in reference to the work of completing the fort:

HEADQUARTERS DEP'T VA. AND NORTH CAROLINA,
IN THE FIELD July 14, 1864.

Colonel Innis, Fort Powhatan:

The commanding general directs that you will state at once by telegraph why you cannot furnish at least 100 men daily for engineer fatigue duty and this fatigue to work all day.

G. WEITZEL,
Brigadier General and Chief Engineer.

Answer.

HEADQUARTERS U. S. FORCES,
FORT POWHATAN, VA., July 15, 1864.

Brigadier General G. Weitzel, Chief of Staff, General:

Your telegram of July 14th received at 7 A. M. this day. I put every available man on engineer fatigue till I received General Order No. 6 from division headquarters requiring me to drill in school of soldier and company at least three hours per day, and one hour additional in battalion drill.

I soon after received from brigade headquarters a time table for these drills dividing them between the A. M. and P. M.

This I soon got modified on application to General Marston so as to allow me to do fatigue duty A. M., and all the drilling P. M.

Since then I have been furnishing in the A. M. all the men for engineer fatigue requested by Lieutenant Baldwin.

I am, general, very respectfully your obedient servant,

G. S. INNIS,
Colonel 133d Regiment Ohio National Guard Commanding Post.

HURRY UP THE FORTIFICATIONS.—

HEADQUARTERS DEP'T OF VA. AND NORTH CAROLINA,
IN THE FIELD July 15, 1864—11:30 A. M.

Colonel Innis, Fort Powhatan:

The general commanding directs that you suspend all drills at your post until all the engineering operations are complete.

You will put every man not on picket or other military duty on fatigue daily, to work at least eight hours per day until the work is finished.

The general commanding further directs that you notify General Marston of this order. The work must be finished at once for the sake of General Grant's whole army.

G. WEITZEL,
Brigadier General.

HEADQUARTERS DEP'T VA. AND NORTH CAROLINA,
IN THE FIELD, July 15, 1864.

Lieutenant Baldwin:

Colonel Innis has been directed to put every available man on engineer fatigue duty to work at least eight hours daily. Drills are suspended. You will push the work to completion at once. Don't let any grass grow under your feet. Get through and then come away with your party.

G. WEITZEL,
Brigadier General.

HEADQUARTERS DEP'T OF VA. AND NORTH CAROLINA,
IN THE FIELD July 25, 1864—6:40 P. M.

Lieutenant Baldwin, First New York Volunteer Engineers: Fort Powhatan:

When will you get through with your work? Please answer at once.

G. WEITZEL,
Brigadier General.

FORT POWHATAN, July 25, 1864.

Brigadier General Weitzel:

Unless I get details more promptly I cannot tell.

This forenoon I had none. This P. M. I required 100 at one o'clock and got only 50 at three P. M. I report to commander of post, but get no more men. There seems to be no system about fatigue detail.

BALDWIN,
Lieutenant Engineers.

JULY 25, 1864—10:35 P. M.
Colonel Innis, Commanding at Fort Powhatan:

How many infantry have you for duty? How many do guard and picket duty daily?

G. WEITZEL,
Brigadier General.

STRENGTH OF GARRISON.—

FORT POWHATAN, July 26, 1864.
Brigadier General Weitzel:

General:—I have infantry for duty as follows: One Hundred and Thirty-third Regiment Ohio National Guard, 504 men, detachment Third Pennsylvania Heavy Artillery, 79 men, Company L. First New York Volunteer Engineers, 59 men; total 642 men. These are employed as follows: Heavy Artillery on fort and fortifications, 47 of engineers on fort and for the magazine, 120 men of the One Hundred and Thirty-third Ohio National Guard on guard and picket duty daily, 120 more are relieved from picket at 10 A. M. daily, generally excused for balance of the day, 150 men One Hundred and Thirty-third Ohio National Guard on daily engineer fatigue on fortifications and magazines about two or three times each week. I have to send from 50 to 150 men to repair U. S. military telegraph line from this place to Swan Point, absent from one to two days each time. Ten to 15 men Ohio National Guard at work on lookout. Yesterday very wet A. M. In P. M. division inspector here inspecting One Hundred and Thirty-third Ohio National Guard.

G. S. INNIS,
Colonel Commanding.

FORT POWHATAN, VA., July 26, 1864.
Brigadier General Weitzel:

General:—Is it expected at department headquarters that I will personally superintend details on engineer fatigue duty or shall I, as heretofore, place such details under the superintendence of Lieutenant Baldwin?

Am I held responsible for any insufficiency of his superintendence?

G. S. INNIS,
Colonel Commanding.

HEADQUARTERS DEP'T VA. AND NORTH CAROLINA,
IN THE FIELD July 26, 1864—10 A. M.
General Innis:

Your dispatch received. Assist the engineers as much as possible and get that work done.

G. WEITZEL,
Brigadier General and Acting Chief of Staff.

INEFFICIENT OFFICER.—

FORT POWHATAN, VA., July 26, 1864.
RECEIVED 8:40 P. M.
General Weitzel:

General:—I consider Lieutenant Baldwin a very

inefficient officer. He sometimes keeps fatigue details waiting from half to one and a half hours before he gets ready to get them to work. One-half the men under proper management could turn off more work.

G. S. INNIS,
Colonel Commanding.

July 26, 1864.

Colonel Innis, Fort Powhatan:

It is only expected that you furnish all details he asks for with promptitude. You are not responsible for his inefficiency.

If you think he is inefficient, it is your duty to report him to these headquarters at once. I can send a better officer, but do not care to make the change just now.

G. WEITZEL,
Brigadier General and Acting Chief of Staff.

A BETTER ONE.—

HEADQUARTERS DEP'T OF VA. AND NORTH CAROLINA,
IN THE FIELD July 29, 1864.

Colonel Innis, Commanding Fort Powhatan:

I have sent you a driving engineer officer. You had better hurry up. General Grant is making movements that may lead to an attack on you. Get your works done quick. Give the engineer officer all your help.

G. WEITZEL,
Brigadier General and Acting Chief of Staff.

The new engineer officer was Captain S. C Eaton, a gentlemanly and energetic man, and the works were soon finished. On making a tour of observation with the Colonel, he commended the works all round and when he came in said, "Colonel, the devil himself couldn't get in here now, even with his wife to help him."

LIFE AT THE FORT.—I will now return to the time of our arrival at the fort. After marching up the hill we pitched our tents, both inside and outside the fort, those outside being within the line of fortifications and of easy access to the fort in case of an attack. Some of the men built up poles or boards a foot or two high and put their tents on top of that, thus making quite a roomy place. We then cleaned up the ground, dug trenches around the tents and along the streets in front of them for drainage, and had quite a respectable camp.

THE NEAT 133d.—In fact the One Hundred and Thirty-third was always noted for the neat manner in which they did everything. When we established our camp at Bermuda Hundred the boys did it so nicely that it attracted the attention of General Foster.

He came galloping by with his staff and when in front of our camp suddenly reined in his horse, almost bringing him on his haunches. "By George!" he exclaimed, "whose camp is this?" "The One Hundred and Thirty-third Ohio, answered some one. "Send your commander to me." Colonel Innis appeared and saluted.

The general said, "Colonel, I want to compliment you on the neatness of your camp. You have the nicest camp in Bermuda Hundred." The Colonel thanked General Foster for the compliment and added, "I ought to be able to lay out a camp for I am a civil engineer when at home."

It is probable that our neatness and dispatch, as shown in this and building our bomb proofs was the reason we were sent to finish up the works at Fort Powhatan.

SOUL INSPIRING WHISKEY.—After we were established at the fort the Post Adjutant complained that he had no suitable place to keep the papers which it was necessary to preserve for reference.

The Colonel requested Captain Von Shilling to send him a man to fix up a cupboard with pigeon holes for this purpose. The man did a nice job, which so pleased the officer that he offered him a dollar for doing it so well. The soldier refused to take it, saying he never charged gentlemen for doing work well, but on leaving remarked that at some other time he might ask a favor of the colonel. On the morning of the Fourth of July this man came to Headquarters with the following request in writing:

Dear Colonel!—Won't you let an old soldier have a canteen full of whiskey to let him know that he has a soul on this glorious Fourth of July?

The James River opposite Fort Powhatan is about three-fourths of a mile wide and one hundred and fourteen feet deep. The tide rises from three to four feet, and when it goes out leaves the marshes above the fort uncovered for a space of several acres. It was much sport for the boys, especially the colored cavalrymen to wade out into the mud with a stick in hand and capture fish which were left behind by the receding tide and were trying to get back to deep water by wriggling along the little rills that were left.

In striking at the fish they would send the thin ooze flying in all directions and got so splattered up that they looked as though they were convalescing from smallpox.

There is a wooden gunboat just below the fort and an ironclad a short distance above, being stationed here to look after matters. We can hear heavy cannonading in the direction of Petersburg, it has been almost a continual roar all day.

GOOD MARKSMANSHIP.—The next day after arriving here (19th) we had dress parade and guard mounting only. We held Sunday-school on the bank of the river below the fort. Some rebels appeared across the river during the afternoon. Our officers could see them plainly through their glasses and concluded to let them have a few doses from the guns of the fort. A shot or two caused them to take refuge behind the house of a rebel Major Dothat living on the road just beyond the river. Captain Von Shilling asked the colonel to let him shoot through the house but the colonel thought there might be women and children within and withheld permission. Von Shilling then said, "I would like to take about three bricks off the top of the chimney." He was told he might try it, and at the next shot the bricks flew, and the rebs got out and skedaddled. Within a short time an old darkey appeared on the bank of the river with a white flag.

A boat was sent and brought him to the fort.

He was taken before the commandant and said, "Massa Colonel, my ole missus say will yo' please stop firin' at de house. De las' shot took tree bricks offen de top ob de chimbly." He was told that as long as they did not harbor the rebs they would be safe, and returned to his home.

Matters settled down to a routine. In addition to the usual roll call, sick call, guard mounting, dress parade, etc., the fatigue detail is made each day, and takes nearly all the well men we have. They work eight hours a day, from 6 to 10, and from 2 to 6, and are completing the fort quite rapidly. Those who are working on the fortifications are furnished a dose of whiskey and quinine each day, so are those working on the bomb proofs.

CHAPTER XIV.

SUPPLY TRAIN ATTACKED.—On the 25th Grant's wagon train and the guard accompanying it are camped on the opposite side of the river. They were attacked by the rebels yesterday in strong force, and had a hard time to save the train, but succeeded, losing quite heavily in both men and horses, and also one gun. The commander of the rear guard said that their horses gave out, and he had ordered 170 of them killed to prevent their falling into the hands of the enemy.

We heard very heavy firing yesterday in the direction they came from, which was no doubt their fight. They were four days coming from White House and intended to reach City Point direct, but were headed off by the enemy and found themselves opposite Powhatan instead of City Point.

GENERAL SHERIDAN HUNGRY.—Colonel Innis went across to pay his respects to General Sheridan who was in command. The general said they had started with only one day's rations and had used up everything. He himself had got so hungry that he offered a soldier a dollar for one hard-tack, telling him it was for the general, but the soldier would not sell it. The rebels seemed very determined in their efforts to capture the train and could have done so had they known the weakness of the escort. They are crossing here now, about eight hundred wagons and twelve thousand troops to guard them. It makes a great army. The mules are very large and fine.

IN A CRITICAL SITUATION.—An incident occurred in connection with this passing army which caused the parties to it considerable anxiety for a time, but eventually it all came out right through the kindness of Secretary of War, Stanton.

It was this: Comrade John B. Waters, of Company C., was very sick at this time. His son was a member of the 13th O. V. I., then with Sheridan's command. The young man paid his father a visit and finding him in a dangerous condition yielded to his filial affection and remained with him without taking the trouble to obtain leave of absence. The elder Waters was taken to Fortress Monroe where he died on August 10th.

His wife had been notified of his sickness and came on in time to meet the regiment at Washington, expecting to find her husband sick, but instead found his body being conveyed home by his son and comrades. In addition to the great shock of this, she learned the position her son was in and was indeed greatly worried. She appealed to the colonel and at his suggestion they went with him to see the Secretary of War, and lay the case before him. Fortune favored them, for they found the busy Secretary alone. It was about nine o'clock in the morning and he had just arrived at his office.

The visitors were shown in at once and after listening to a recital of of the circumstances this brusque and busy man said, "Well, I will fix that," and he at once wrote young Waters a furlough for sixty days, dating it back so as to cover the time he had been absent without leave. Handing it to him he said, "This will fix matters all right for the time you have lost and give you an opportunity to accompany your mother home and recuperate your health which I see is not good, and when your furlough expires you can rejoin your regiment and do your duty manfully." You may be sure that Waters and his mother were greatly relieved and thanked Mr. Stanton sincerely for his kindness in extricating the son from his dangerous position.

WILSON'S RAID.—On the 30th we heard heavy firing in the direction of Petersburg and next day there came into our camp a good many of our Union soldiers from that direction. Some of them are badly wounded.

PECULIAR WOUNDS.—Among them two Lieutenant Colonels, who, to all appearances, are shot directly through the body, but they are walking about and the surgeons say that the balls passed around under the skin, blistering all the way, and came out on the opposite side, it being a very curious coincidence that two were shot in the same way. They both said when they were shot they fell and thought they were killed, but found after a little that they could get up. They then got on their horses and came in with the troops. One boy of about seventeen years had fourteen bullet and buckshot holes in him and yet was in a fair way to recover.

These men say they started twelve days ago with

eight thousand men went around Petersburg tore up the different railroads, burned depots, government stores and destroyed six thousand stand of arms for the enemy. But when they got within a few miles of our post they encountered the rebels strongly entrenched and ready for them. They had a hard fight and had to destroy all their guns before they left them. Some of the gunners would shed tears while relating the loss of their guns.

This was the firing we heard, and the reason it sounded so loud was that it was only eight miles from us.

The men who came in here showed the effects of the hard service they had gone through.

PLANTATION DARKIES.—Quite a large number of contrabands came about this time. They were very ignorant and most of them very black and said they had been looking for the Yankees for a long time. They were dressed in all sorts of clothing. One shiny black fellow had on a black cloth prince Albert coat and pants, the latter tucked into a pair of officer's cavalry boots, and a soldier cap. Another had a pair of faded jeans pants, a cotton shirt, and nothing else except a rag on his sore toe.

These two were leaders in a dance which they all indulged in on parade ground. The music was furnished by an old tin messpan, with one patting juber, and an old white-headed darkey lining out a hymn in the old-fashioned Methodist way.

They all entered into the dance with a great deal of energy, and seemed as happy as if they were at home, surrounded by all the comforts of life. But they certainly did not know much about comfort, judging by what one of them said.

He was told that he might take some straw and occupy a vacant tent. He answered, "Oh, no use goin' to so much trubble as dat foh a niggah! I allus sleeps in de fence connah to home."

MARRIAGE NOT A FAILURE.—Some of them had never gone through the formality of being married and now wished to avail themselves of the privilege of being married by a minister, and to have their children christened. The chaplain was in a quandary which to do first, until the colonel helped him out by suggesting that up north the marriage usually came first. About twenty couples were legally united, but the spectators did not make haste to salute the brides as we do at home. All waited for the chaplain and colonel to take the lead, but in this solitary instance they lacked courage.

In 1893, while surveying in Clinton Township, Franklin County, Ohio., Colonel Innis came near a house occupied by colored people. An old colored woman, weighing about three hundred pounds, waddled up to the fence, and addressed him thus:

"Lawd, honey! Yo' doesn't know me, does yo'?"

"No, I do not remember you."

"Well, honey! I'se one ob dem dat was married at de fort when yous was down dere. Ise a good cook an I want yo' to come in an take dinner wid me, an put your hoss in de stable dar."

"We brought dinner and horse feed with us, but if you will make coffee, we will bring our dinner and put it on your table and we'll all have dinner together." Which was done to the delight of the old woman.

CHANGE OF DIET.—Our rations here are varied quite a good deal. A bakery has been established and furnishes us with soft bread every second day. The boys go out and gather blackberries and the baker makes them pies on the shares.

Our cooks were not professionals, and I have not heard that the Astors or Vanderbilts have since the war secured the services of any of them for their own private use, but they usually managed to have the pork and beans done so we could eat it, especially when we had been on picket or fatigue duty.

You will all remember what a profusion of silverware we had on the table, and how careful we were not to soil the table cloth.

Of course we always had napkins and flowers on the table.

Then how attentive and deferential the waiters always were.

Sometimes the boys would get tired of so much style and would endeavor to cook for themselves, and they most all used about the same ingredients for their dishes, viz: Hard-tack, rice, beans, and sowbelly. The first and last more constantly than the others.

When you take half a dozen hard-tack, put them in your haversack and pound them with the butt end of your musket, soak them in water a while, and then fry them in the grease from the previously fried pork, you have a fine dish, and glad to get it. *That is if you are hungry.* The hard-tack were nice to eat dry, they polished your teeth so well.

The Sanitary Commission sends tea, pickles, onions, etc., of which we get a taste once in a while. There are hundreds of acres of neglected land about here which is grown up with brush and blackberry bushes, and it is easy enough to get all the berries one wants.

SUPERFLUOUS.—One of the soldiers' aid societies, ever mindful of the boys in the field, thought they would send us something nice, and what would be better than canned berries to the men who were living on hard-tack, etc., so they sent a fine lot of them, which reached us in good condition, but just when we had a surfeit of them. We had just been wishing our friends could be in our blackberry patch a little while. But their kindness of heart was shown anyhow.

While gathering blackberries, the boys find cannon balls and shells scattered here and there among the bushes. They were thrown by our gunboats when Fort Powhatan was captured from the rebels a month ago.

FORAGING.—Quite a little foraging has been done by small parties of our men since we have been here, and mutton, vegetables of different kinds, as peas, potatoes, cabbage, and the like, are secured to help vary the diet. Beeves are killed also and we get fresh meat now and then.

During one of the foraging expeditions, while the soldiers were digging potatoes on the Harrison plantation, four miles down the river from the fort, one of them using a pick to dig with struck something which sounded hollow, and on digging a little further unearthed a box containing between $300.00 and $400.00 in gold and silver money. As soon as he had broken into the box enough to see what it was, he called, Hello, boys! Just come here and see what I have found. There was at once a scramble for the treasure, and while all were securing what they could, the finder was crowded out of the ring and did not get any. He complained to the officers of his loss, but could not be helped any in recovering his treasuretrove. He would perhaps be wiser on another similar occasion.

Some of these foragers ran great risks. A couple of the most active foragers in the regiment belonging to Company H., A. G. McKee and Scott or "Scotty", had secured a promise from some of the native young women to meet them at a certain log house, about four miles from the fort, with chickens and other produce to exchange for coffee, tea and such other commodities as the boys could bring.

Inviting two or three others to join them (among them being a lieutenant of the colored troops), and securing passes from the commandant, they set out for the designated place, anticipating a lively flirtation with the fair rebels, as well as a good commercial deal.

In due time they reached the log house in a small clearing, but the girls had not yet arrived. Some sheep in the field about the house were quietly nibbling the grass and seemed to be about what the foragers "needed." So they sallied out with revolvers in hand, but before they got within pistol shot a troop of U. S. cavalry entered the clearing by a road through the woods and turned to the right, into the shade just about where they would be hit if the sheep were missed. The boys retreated to the hut and were promptly put under arrest by the commander of the cavalry, which proved to be the First New York Mounted Rifles, but were released upon showing their passes.*

About this time they were startled by shooting in the edge of the woods about seventy-five feet in the rear of the cabin.

It proved that the girls had not come themselves, but had kindly sent a half dozen of their rebel friends to gobble up the foragers. The timely appearance of the cavalry saved them from capture.

In the skirmish one rebel was killed and five captured, one of the latter it is said, the cavalry hung.

The boys were greatly angered at the job the girls had put up on them and in a few days returned to burn the house, but were informed that a squad of rebel cavalry was near, so they made tracks for the fort as if the devil was after them.

We get our mail twice or three times a week, about five or six days after the letters are written.

THE "GLORIOUS FOURTH."—July 4th. We celebrated the day by having regimental review and erecting a flag-pole in the fort, on which was run up

*Although the commander of the cavalry released the boys, he sent a note to Colonel Innis telling where he found them, and that it was a dangerous place for them to be. The boys had secured their passes under pretense of going to pick berries just outside of our picket lines, but within sight of them.

the stars and stripes. A salute of thirty-four guns was fired, and the boats in the river were decked out with flags and bunting in honor of the day.

A newspaper correspondent was so soundly asleep that he did not hear the salute, and wrote home to his paper that there was no demonstration at the fort.

FIGHTING WHISKEY.—Captain Von Shilling asked the commandant of the post for a requisition for two gallons of whiskey so he could give each of his men a drink as they had been working hard on the magazines etc., and wished to celebrate the day. On procuring the fluid he mustered his men and began at one end and passed down the line, giving each man his treat. Before he reached the other end the first men served began to get hilarious and one of them struck another with a bucket, injuring him severely.

The wounded man was taken to the surgeon to have his scalp stitched up, and the one who assaulted him was, by order of the captain, tied spread-eagle fashion to a cannon wheel. He was left there till sundown, and it was the captain's intention to leave him there all night, but the colonel thought he had been punished enough and ordered him released. This was probably some of the fighting whiskey that General Grant was said to drink.

UNDRESS UNIFORM.—The days were extremely hot so that most of the boys ran around camp when not on duty with only shirt and drawers on during the middle of the day, but the nights were cold enough to require the use of an overcoat.

On the 7th a detail from different companies under command of Captain Fisher went down to Wm. B. Harrison's plantation and brought back eleven head of horses and a jenny.

One of the jolly boys of the regiment George Merion, claimed the jenny as his steed and with nothing on but shirt and drawers, bestrode the meek little creature and rode about the camp proclaiming to every one that he was starting out to meet the entire Confederate cavalry and would soon put them to rout. The ludicrous appearance of the outfit called forth shouts of laughter on all sides.

CHAPTER XV.

DROWNED.—One of the men belonging to the artillery was drowned while in swimming, and his body was not recovered until next day, although a cannon was fired on the river bank in the hope of raising it.

Another body was found in the river the day after this one and proved to be that of a man who had been missing some time and was thought to be of unsound mind.

A SAD ROMANCE.—Connected with this death was one of the many thousand romances growing out of the war.

The story is as follows: The young man was engaged to be married, and when the militia was ordered out, called on his fiancee and urged that they be married at once. The young lady, while expressing the strongest affection for him, was influenced by her parents and friends and thought it would be best to wait till he returned from the service, as it would not be long, and then there would be no interruption of their happiness. He yielded and marched away with the regiment, buoyed up by the prospect of soon returning to claim his bride.

He received the occasional letters that had been promised, and everything seemed to be well, until about the time we reached Fort Powhatan. Here he received an anonymous letter stating that the object of his affections had been married on a certain day. The letter described the wedding dinner and ceremony, dress of the bride, gave names of guests present and everything with such minuteness as to seem like reality.

The poor fellow was distracted with grief and went with the letter to the colonel, who was well acquainted with both parties.

Colonel Innis told him to pay no attention to the letter, that he knew the lady and did not believe a word of it.

This seemed to satisfy the lover for a time, but soon he was worrying again, and not long after was missing. The finding of his body showed what the sequel of the anonymous letter was.

The letter was in all probability written as a joke, but it was death to the recipient. No one knows what agony he suffered from some one's mischievousness, until he finally sought relief in the waters of the James.

OUR DEADLIEST ENEMY.—The rebels were not the only foes we had to contend with at this place.

Along toward the middle of July a good many of the men were troubled with diarrhea, which was quite obstinate and rapidly weakened them. We also had another foe whose approach was more insiduous, whose attacks were harder to repel, took more time to recover from, and was in every way more discouraging.

The Malarial Typhoid Fever, peculiar to the James River, was this foe. Nearly three hundred men of our regiment were on the sick list with this terrible disease at the same time. At one time only 333 were fit for duty. The men would first complain of feeling tired and stiff, muscles sore, headache and dizziness, much like ague coming on, then a slight fever would appear in the afternoons, getting worse and lasting longer each day, till finally it would be continuous and the patient delirious, and he would be a very sick man. This would last for three or four weeks, when the patient would usually be able to walk about a little, looking like a yellow ghost, reeling as he went and feeling dizzy and miserable as could be imagined. He would of course keep on drinking swamp water from the spring (?) which supplied the garrison, and would soon be down again with a relapse unless he took medicine as regularly as he ate his meals. If he did this he might keep just about so. If he neglected his quinine down he went. The usual bill of fare at this time was hardtack and sowbelly, with quinine for dessert (after blackberries were gone).

Several attempts were made to get better water by digging wells in several places. Some wells which were dug along the banks of the river gave a supply which seemed a little better than that from the spring. There was a fine spring outside the picket lines, but that was too far off and seemed too dangerous to be utilized, though several times barrels of the water were brought in by guarded parties.

The stoutest and most robust men in the command seemed to be the first victims of the fever. Among those we lost by it was Major Joseph M. Clark, a most estimable man and a genial comrade, and

Captain Thomas Lilley, a Mexican veteran, a very efficient officer and agreeable man.

Major Clark was taken to Fortress Monroe, where he died.

Captain Lilley had been sent to Bermuda Hundred to the field hospital there, but it was intended to remove him to Fortress Monroe. He was taken on board the boat in the evening to start in the morning, but he died during the night.

Many of the men went home from service about as miserable as they could be, from the effects of these diseases, some of them being affected for years with chronic liver and stomach trouble and diarrhea.

GLOOMY THOUGHTS.—When a man got too sick for duty or to eat his rations and could only sit around and think of his ailments and wonder how things were going on at home, he was pretty apt to get blue and homesick. He knew that he had left home on short notice and did not have time to arrange his affairs, consequently he had to leave his farming to his wife and children, or his store or shop in the care of clerks or apprentices. This fact and his sickness made him feel as if he was about broke up.

When they were well all the members of the regiment, though conscious of the sacrifices they had made, accepted the situation cheerfully and manfully and stood up to their work bravely. They could not help thinking sometimes how nice it would be if they could only look in on the folks at home for a little while, and straighten up business matters somewhat. They could then come back contented to serve out the balance of their term, or longer if needed, but there was no chance for a furlough.

Among the kind offices to be performed for the boys when they were sick was that of writing letters to friends at home, and it was a duty which was done cheerfully by all who were called upon, but no one excelled our (Rev.) Lieutenant Whitehead, whose letters carried such comfort to the friends of sick and dying comrades, that he will long be remembered. Some of his letters were so prized that they were printed and framed by the families who received them, and still remain as reminders of his goodness of heart.

The sickest men and those who were likely to be sick for some time, were put on steamboats and sent to the hospital at Fortress Monroe, where more convenient and permanent arrangements had been made for the care of sick and wounded, than could be had in the field.

Our own field hospital would of course accommodate only a small number, and it is not customary to keep on hand any great amount of medicines, so that our supply got pretty low. Another good reason for sending away the sick was that we were liable to be attacked at any time.

ON THE ALERT.—We are continually reminded that war exists in our vicinity by the heavy firing up the rivers in the direction of Petersburg and Richmond, and we anxiously wait for the time when we will have to repel a rebel attack on our post. Quite frequently the rebels will station themselves on the river bank above or below this place, plant a battery and begin firing on every boat that passes up or down.

On the Fourth of July they appeared with a battery at Wilcox's Wharf, between three and four miles up the river on the opposite side, and began firing on some transports that were passing up loaded with hay and grain for Grant's and Butler's armies. There were nine of the boats, three abreast. The rebel aim seemed poor, for many of the shots fell into the water around the boats, but did not do much damage. Only one hole was made of any consequence, and the boat's crew soon patched that up.

The rebels were in plain view from the fort, and as soon as they began firing we of course wanted to be at them, but it was out of our reach, for by the time we could land a force on the other side of the river and march to where they were they could have the boats sunk and be gone. So our commander ordered Captain Von Shilling to try the cannon of the fort on them. He said, "I don't believe we can reach them, but I will try." We had two guns, one a brass thirty-two pounder, the other a steel gun much larger. The brass piece was tried first, and the shot struck the water in direct line toward the rebs, but only about two-thirds of the way to them. The steel gun was then loaded and the shot went nearly to them. The colonel said, "Put in a double charge, captain." "I am afraid it will spoil the gun," was answered. "Will it hurt any of us?" "Oh no! but it will likely crack the gun." "Well, try it! Uncle Sam will get us another."

So a double charge was put in with a shell, and

when the gun was fired, those who had their eyes on the rebs saw men, horses, and cannon suddenly fly into the air, and then in wild confusion they lit out for other parts.

The shell had gone under the gun platform, and exploded just at the right time to be most effective.

THEY'RE SLOW, BUT LOOK OUT WHEN THEY GET THERE.—The gunboat stationed below the fort started up the river to attack this battery, but to the eyes of the anxious and excited soldiers at the fort it seemed to hardly move, and many were the exclamations of disgust at its slowness. Our shots drove the rebs away before the boat got half way there. These gunboats soon rout the rebels when they happen to be on hand, but the Johnnies take advantage of their absence, as the boats have to patrol the river up and down for several miles.

See follwing dispatches.

July 13, 1864.

Major General B. F. Butler :

There is a rebel battery firing on our transports at Wilcox's Wharf at the bend of the river just above this place. No gunboat here.

G. S. INNIS,
Colonel Commanding.

A gunboat happened to be just around the bend and attended to them, as see,

BERMUDA, July 13, 1864.

Major General Butler :

I have just come up the river from near Wilcox's

Wharf. Captain Fitch with the army gunboat Parke was near there when a section of artillery fired into the transports this P. M., and shelled them out, afterward landing a party to ascertain where they were gone.

C. K. GRAHAM,
Brigadier General.

FORT POWHATAN, VA., August 3, 1864.
Major General Butler:

There is a rebel battery at Wilcox's Wharf firing on our transports.

G. S. INNIS,
Colonel.

ANOTHER COMPLIMENT.—During the early part of August the ironclad lying near the fort was ordered up the river. Before leaving the Lieutenant Commander in command of her came on shore to bid our commander good-bye. He said, "Colonel, I do not wish to flatter your command, but since the 133d has been here things have been conducted in a more military way than at any time since I have been here, and your camp is the cleanest and nicest about Bermuda Hundred."

So the time wore on, each day being enlivened by some incident of soldier life, a march out along the telegraph line, a scout after some rebel detachment reported to be near, or other duty besides the usual guard and fatigue duty.

CHAPTER XVI.

WELCOME VISITORS.—About the latter part of July the wives of Colonel Innis and Lieutenant Colonel Ewing came to the fort on a visit and stayed a couple of weeks. This was a great pleasure to the whole regiment. Many were acquainted with the ladies and could thus obtain direct news from home, while the others could hear in a general way how matters were at home, which was a good deal of satisfaction, besides the ladies showed a good many kindnesses to the sick, which were greatly needed, for at this time the malarial fever was at about its worst.

The marshy country around the fort, heated up by the fierce rays of the sun through the day, rendered the air almost unfit to be breathed, and the sick were reported by the dozens.

SIGNAL TOWER.—Our men worked on a lookout and signal station, 96 feet high, which they completed late in July. By means of this tower the country for miles around could be continuously watched through the day and signals conveyed from the station at Fort Pocahontas, eight miles below on the river, and repeated here to the one at City Point, ten miles up the river. By means of telescopes these signals, communicated by flags by day and torches by night, could be seen and read, thus conveying information as quickly and as accurately as by telegraph, or as could now be done by telephone.

General Butler had one of these towers on the line of his works near Point of Rocks, nearly two hundred feet high, and from the top of it he could look over the rebel works for three or four miles, and could see their movements along the road between Richmond and Petersburg. It was his custom to be drawn up to the top in a basket by means of a windlass each day between 10 and 12 o'clock when the atmosphere was clearest, and take observations for himself. Beauregard had observed this proceeding and telegraphed for a Whitworth gun to destroy this lookout, and it was sent him by express with the necessary ammunition. Accordingly a couple of days afterward when General Butler went up to take a look at the rebs they sent their compliments at the tower in the way of a shot from their Whitworth gun, the projectile of which is nearly two feet long and makes a terrible shrieking as it flies through the air.

Butler knew that if a shot hit one of the corner posts he would take a fall of a couple of hundred feet, but he remained and signalled for two batteries to be brought, and then from his perch directed their fire one after the other, till they got the range.

The rebs in the meantime fired three or four shots and were getting nearer the mark, but when our guns got their adjustment the whole twelve opened at once, and in a few minutes the Whitworth was knocked completely out and was never heard from again.

WE GO AFTER THE REBS.—From the time

the fortifications were completed we had no fatigue
duty to perform and our own work was comparatively easy, but in the early part of August the rebels
became more troublesome, cutting the wire oftener
and finally appearing in some force near Cabin Point,
as shown by the following dispatches:

FORT POWHATAN, August 6, 1864.
General B. F. Butler :

I think there is a considerable force of rebels between here and Swan Point, led by Roger A. Pryor.
Two of colored cavalry repairing telegraph line were
killed last night and one missing. The line however
is in working order.

G. S. INNIS,
Colonel 133d Ohio National Guard Regiment Commanding Post.

FORT POWHATAN, VA., August 6, 1864.
*Major General Butler, Commanding Department of Virginia and
North Carolina :*

General:—Negroes say they saw at least 100
men. Their horses were hitched in the woods and
the men were formed along the road in a ditch or riflepits. One free negro said they captured him, took
him into their lines, showed him their men and told
him they had 80 or 100 men. This was last evening
about sunset. This morning I cannot find or hear of
them. If I can find out anything certain about them
I will telegraph you. Several citizens have recently
come in voluntarily and asked to be allowed to take
the oath of allegience to the Government of the
United States. Shall I have it administered to all

that ask it if I believe them to be acting in good faith?
I am very respectfully, general, your most obedient servant,

G. S. INNIS,
Colonel Commanding Post.

A movement was projected against this force, having for its intention to get them between two detachments of our forces, but General Marston did not get transportation soon enough and was blamed by General Butler, as per following dispatch.

BUTLER SCOLDS.—

HEADQUARTERS, August 10, 1864—10:20 P. M.
Brigadier General Marston, Fort Powhatan:

I desired Colonel Innis to cooperate with General Graham in a movement upon the enemy near Cabin Point and to pursue them down to Swan Point.

Graham landed at daybreak. You stopped the march of Colonel Innis until 10:45 by saying, "Don't move till I come, I will be there in an hour. Do you not get up to make movements till 10:45? It is a little later in the morning than I am accustomed to see my officers move. Please explain.

BENJAMIN F. BUTLER,
Major General.

General Marston explained as follows:

HEADQUARTERS FIRST BRIGADE THIRD DIVISION
TENTH ARMY CORPS,
FORT POWHATAN, VA., August 11, 1864,
Major General Butler:

On the 9th day of August, at 2:30 P. M., I received the following dispatch from Colonel Innis, commanding at Fort Powhatan:

"A white nigger has just reported to me that there are three companies of cavalry within three miles of this fort, also a large infantry force on the Surry Court House road.

He says 3,000. I think the 400 or 500 I spoke to you about yesterday. I sent out thirty or forty cavalry to repair the telegraph line this A. M., but they were driven in. What shall I do?"

At 3 P. M. I sent the following to Colonel Innis:

"Keep a sharp lookout, but don't risk capture or surprise."

Deeming it important to destroy or capture the rebel force that was interrupting the telegraph at 3:45 P. M. I telegraphed to Captain Pitkin at City Point to send me a steamer that night to enable me to cross the river with a part of my force at this post, to which I received no reply until between 7 and 8 o'clock in the morning of the 10th instant, when the steamer called for reported.

My purpose was to send a section of my light battery and about 150 men to Fort Powhatan in the evening and during the night land about 250 men below Cabin Point and endeavor to surprise the rebels at daylight this morning by a simultaneous movement of both detachments.

At 9:30 A. M., August 10th, I received the following dispatch from Colonel Innis:

"We are about sending out all our available force. In case we are driven in can I depend on you for assistance?"

To which I replied:

"Make no movement until I come, will be with you in an hour."

In less than one hour I was at Fort Powhatan, and then and there first learned that General Graham had sent a force down the river, and that Colonel Innis had been requested to cooperate with him. I immediately directed Colonel Innis to send out all the men he could possibly spare and sent back to Wilson's Landing for 375 men, 100 of whom I directed to remain at Fort Powhatan and 275 I sent to reinforce the detachment sent forward by Colonel Innis. A part of the force marched as far as Cabin Point and scouted the country about there, arrested several citizens, who, with one exception, persisted that no more than six rebel soldiers had been seen recently in that neighborhood. From one party they learned that about seventy-five rebel cavalry had that morning gone off on the Blackwater road. They found the telegraph line down at several points, but not broken. Between 8 and 9 o'clock the force returned to Fort Powhatan.

I enclose herewith a report of Lieutenant Swain, which accounts for the fact that no communication was received from Fort Powhatan on the night of the 9th instant. To your remark about not getting up to make movements till 10:45 I have no reply to make, feeling that the same was uncalled for and unjust.

I have the honor to be very respectfully your obedient servant,

GILMAN MARSTON,
Brigadier General of Volunteers.

Lieutenant Swain reported that smoke in the atmosphere prevented torch signals being seen, the distance being nearly eight miles.

BUSHWHACKERS.—Although on this expedition no rebel force was encountered, our men who lagged behind on the return march were fired on by bushwhackers and returned the fire, but none of our men were hurt.

WE LEAVE FORT POWHATAN.—We did not know how long we were to be kept in the service, but thought our time was nearly up, and began to expect orders to leave at almost any time, and when the following order came it was received with great satisfaction.

HEADQUARTERS TENTH ARMY CORPS,
IN THE FIELD August 10, 1864.

SPECIAL ORDERS }
No. 98.   }

5. The One Hundred and Thirtieth Ohio National Guard will proceed without delay to Fort Powhatan, relieving the One Hundred and Thirty-third Ohio National Guard now on duty there. The One Hundred and Thirty-third Ohio National Guard, upon being relieved, will proceed upon the same transport to Washington, D. C.

By command of Major General Birney.

ED. W. SMITH,
Assistant Adjutant-General.

The colonel had reported to General Butler that we had so many sick that it would be very inconvenient to take them on a boat crowded with noisy soldiers, and asked for a hospital boat. Butler telegraphed to Baltimore and the authorities in command there impressed a peach boat the "Mina" and sent her to convey our sick.

TAMING A REBEL.—The captain was a rebel sympathizer and did not relish this service a bit, but dared not disobey orders. He, however, took every opportunity to make himself disagreeable, and carried it so far that the colonel ordered a squad of men to pitch him overboard into the James.

He now realized the situation and begged for mercy, which was granted. During the rest of the trip he behaved himself with some show of respect for every one on board.

About 10 o'clock on August 11th, the steamers United States and Mina arrived at the fort with the 130th O. V. I., which was to relieve us.

We were at once ordered to strike tents and pack up, which we were not slow to do. At once everything was hurry and bustle, and about 4 o'clock we went aboard the United States, the sick being placed on the Mina. When the boats got out into the river the boys gave three hearty cheers, and our fifes and drums played "When Johnny comes marching home."

The weather was very hot, but when we got down the river a piece the banks were low and the breeze got a chance to strike us, making it very pleasant.

The country had the same deserted appearance we noticed on going up the river.

We passed Fortress Monroe about 11 o'clock at night.

August 12th, at about six o'clock in the morning, we turned from the bay into the Potomac River. It was quite cool in the early morning, but soon got so warm that the boys stretched their tents over their heads, which helped a little, and yet it was so hot that the perspiration streamed from every pore.

The night had been a very uncomfortable one on account of being so crowded on the boat. The men lay in every possible shape to find room, some even letting their legs hang over the sides of the boat. Our journey up the Potomac was uneventful and in a few hours more we were once again in the Capital of the Nation and the boys' faces beamed with smiles at the change. For nearly four months we have scarcely seen any one but soldiers, and these living in a rough and tumble sort of a way that does not seem at all like the way people should live, but now that we have got back from the seat of war and see women and children again it seems more like civilization.

CHAPTER XVII.

BACK TO WASHINGTON.—We disembarked and marched to the Soldiers' Home, where we got supper.

Three of our sick men died on the boat, coming up. All the rest who were not able to accompany the regiment home were sent to the different hospitals.

THE PRESIDENT WANTS TO SEE US.—In the evening we were drawn up to go to the White House, on the invitation of President Lincoln, but a furious rainstorm prevented our attendance.

We found the 150th O. N. G. here and they looked very clean and well kept. They must have had a very easy time as compared with our regiment.

EVERY ONE KIND TO SOLDIERS.—The Sanitary Commission sent each company of our command a bushel of good peaches, which seemed delicious to us.

The people of the North were full of patriotism and sent liberal donations to this commission to be distributed to the soldiers. Nearly every family in the land sent one or more of its number to the field and the hearts of those who remained at home were filled with love for all who were in the Union army, and they were ever ready to do them a kindness.

Postmaster General Dennison was very kind to

the members of the 133d, even going so far as to authorize drafts to be drawn on him for money that any member of the regiment might need.

After we boarded the cars for home at Washington City, a Quaker lady approached an officer of our regiment and said, "Thee looks as if thee had come from the front." "Yes," was the reply, "we have come from in front of Petersburg and Richmond."

"Thee looks as if a little money might be useful to thee. I have twenty dollars in my purse which thee is welcome to," and she offered a twenty dollar bill, which the officer declined, saying, "No, I thank you! We are now where we can get all the money we need. Keep that for some one who may not be so fortunate."

GO HOME.—On Sunday morning, August 14th, at 4 o'clock, we were ordered to pack up and be ready to move. We waited till 9 o'clock, when we got started, and at 2 o'clock we got to Baltimore. Here we were treated to a good dinner of corned beef and bread and excellent coffee, and then marched a mile and a half to the other depot. One man died on the train coming to Baltimore.

We boarded our train and pulled out of Baltimore just about dusk. The moon shone brightly and gave a beautiful appearance to the country as we glided along on the cars.

All along the road the people turn out and greet us with cheers and all the usual signs of patriotism.

The morning of August 15th found us within forty-five miles of Harrisburg, Pa. Here we were divided into two trains, having come so far on a single train. Passing through Harrisburg we kept on, and about noon arrived at Altoona. Here we got dinner and had two extra engines attached to our train, as the grades among these mountains are very steep and the road very crooked. It seems sometimes as if we were going right back the way we came. After a while we got over the ridge of the mountains and reached the down grade and then made very fast time.

A GOOD SUPPER.—We reached Pittsburg about 7 o'clock P. M., got off the train and went to the Soldiers' Home, where in a clean, nice dining room they gave us the best supper we had seen since we left home. We had bread and *butter*, coffee, *good water*, dried beef, tomatoes, cabbage, pickles, butter crackers and an apple a piece. The boys showed their appreciation of the good things by giving three cheers and singing some army songs. We then marched about half a mile to the depot and were given passenger cars to ride in this time.

It seems that the nearer home we get the better we find things. Then, as now, Ohio was the best state in the Union.

We got to Alliance about 6 o'clock in the morning, and from here on to Crestline the country looks fine. Our colonel telegraphed to different towns ahead to know if they could feed the regiment, directing them to telegraph their answer to the next station ahead of us. Each place answered that they could not, till Crestline was asked. The answer now was, "Yes!" We got there about 1 o'clock, and having had nothing to eat since we left Pittsburg last night, the men were nearly famished. Consequently they did full justice to the dinner provided for as here.

Boarding our train again we proceeded toward Columbus, where we arrived about 4 o'clock, with hearts beating with joy to be at home and among friends once more.

A GREAT WELCOME.—There were thousands of people at the depot to welcome us, and they fairly went wild with joy as we alighted from the cars. Everybody embraced everybody else, and then shook hands all round and cried and laughed, and gave other evidence of the emotion that possessed them.

SOME SAD HEARTS.—There were some hearts though that were sad amid all this tumult of gladness.

Twenty-seven of the brave comrades who went away with us full of manly pride and patriotism, to serve their country, had died, and to their families there was no glad home-coming. These friends could not participate in the general rejoicing, but could only mourn for the loved ones they had given as a sacrifice to preserve the Union. Some sick comrades had been left at Washington, but their friends were hopeful that they would soon come home too.

When greetings were over for the time, the regiment fell in and was formed in open order and the food and delicacies brought by our friends was passed along the lines.

WE WERE TOO FULL.—The display of eatables would have tempted any hungry man, but unfortunately we were in no condition to do justice to the offering. We had nearly starved from Pittsburg to Crestline, and at the latter place had eaten so heartily that we lost our appetites. At the Soldiers' Home, which stood just south of the railroad on the west side of High street, we were also invited in to dinner, but could not accept.

Fresh horses had been provided for the field officers.

OUR GRAND PARADE.—After supper the regiment was re-formed and a parade of the City Fire Department and the local military organizations took place in honor of our return.

We then marched to the State House, while cannon were fired and all the bells of the city clanged out their glad welcome.

Here Dr. G. Volney Dorsey (State Treasurer) welcomed us back in a stirring patriotic speech, after which the regiment was dismissed till morning, and scattered to their homes or those of their friends.

On the 17th the regiment assembled and at 11 o'clock marched out to Camp Chase in order to be mustered out as soon as the necessary forms could be complied with, and papers made out. The men were not under much restraint now, and ran about almost at will.

OUT. On the 20th we were mustered out by Captain Brand, of the 18th U. S. Infantry, having been in Uncle Sam's service one hundred and ten days.

GOODBYE, BOYS.—The boys had already prepared for their departure, and all that was left to be done was to bid farewell to each other, and this caused many heartpangs, for though our term of service was short, it was long enough to allow the formation of that feeling of fraternity which is so strong between soldiers who have lived and marched together, and stood with elbows touching in times of danger and death.

The memory of that service will linger with us through life.

To our surviving comrades we extend a heartfelt greeting whenever we meet them.

To the memory of those who fell we drop tears of sorrow.

133RD REGIMENT OHIO VOLUNTEER INFANTRY.

Field and Staff, and Companies A, E, F, G, H and K mustered in by Major Cravens, and Companies B, C, D and I by Captain Otis, May 6, 1864, at Camp Chase, Ohio. Mustered out August 20, 1864, by Captain E. E. Brand, 18th Infantry U. S. A., at Camp Chase, Ohio.

FIELD AND STAFF.

Colonel,
Gustavus S. Innis.

Lieutenant-Colonel,
William Ewing.

Major,
Joseph M. Clark.

Surgeon,
Chauncey P. Landon.

Assistant Surgeons,
Robert M. McConnell.
David Ridenour.

Adjutant,
George W. Hayden.

Regimental Quartermaster,
Carl N. Bancroft.

Chaplain,
James Mitchell.

Sergeant-Major,
Wilson Hume.

Quartermaster Sergeant,
William Chandler.

Commissary Sergeant,
Adam R. Innis.

Hospital Stewards,
John E. Powell,
William Miller.

Principal Musicians,
Edward Harris,
James Strasburgh,
Henry W. Field.

COMPANY A.

Captain,
Joseph Steely.

First Lieutenant,
James Watermire.

Second Lieutenant,
Jefferson H. Darrah.

First Sergeant,
Orville R. Pegg.

Sergeants,

William W. Woods,
Francis H. Switzer,

Jeremiah Greer,
John W. H. Morrison,

Corporals,

William Webster,
Wilson Ludivck.
Henry H. Miller,
George Woods,

Stewart Stradley,
Joseph Webster,
Leroy ~. Lafferty,
Thomas A. Fritter.

Musicians,

Nelson Kidney,

Charles White.

Wagoner,
John Wilson.

Privates.

Babcock, Jacob
Bacon, John
Beard, Ira H.
Beigle, Alva
Beigle, David.
Brown, William
Brown, Daniel H.
Bull, Heman.
Butterbergh, George
Cameron, Samuel
Cameron, Joseph
Cramer, John
  Sent from hospital at David's Island, New York Harbor, to Columbus, O., Sept, 8, 1864, for muster-out.
Cramer, Adam
Crut, Michael
Cunmans, David
Drake, William
  Died June 8, 1864, at New Creek, W. Va.
Drake, John W.
  Died July 4, 1864, at New Creek, W. Va.
Dupes, Adam
Elder, Sylvester
Furguson, John
Furguson, Samuel
Ferreter, Richard
Garner, William
  Died Aug. 7, 1864.
Geisinger, George W.
Hanel, Henry
Harris, Samuel
  Died June 6, 1864, at New Creek, W. Va.
Harris, Albert
Hashberger, Coffinberly
Hodge, G. W. S.
Houston Hugh
Huntly, John
Icenberger, John.
Innis, Robert.

Innis, Adam R.
  Promoted to Com. Sergeant May 2, 1864.
Kirkpatrick, John.
Lakin, John W. P.
Leese Terrace T.
Linderman, Christian.
Martin, Christian.
Miller, John C.
Miller, Jackson.
Mock, Joseph.
Moore, Elijah A.
Moore, Henry.
Musgrove, William.
Newel, Joseph P.
Ransbottom, Henry.
  Died July 30, 1864, at Fortress Monroe, Va.
Reader, Jacob.
Rean, George.
Reigle, Elias.
Rinehart, Valentine.
Robins, Joseph W.
Rose, John A.
Rose, Daniel W.
Rothgeb, Elijah.
Rothworth, Amos.
Sabastian, George W.
Sabastian, Joseph.
Shively, John.
Sims, John.
Strickland, George.
Super, Michael.
Switser, John.
Thomson, John.
Thomson, Marion
Umbaugh, William H.
Waltimire, William J.
Wart, John
Webster, F. A.
Woods, N. B.
Woods, E. H.
Wolford, John

COMPANY B.

Captain,
Job Wilson.

First Lieutenant,
Sylvester W. Ranney.

Second Lieutenant,
Oliver Marion.

First Sergeant,
George Wagner.

Sergeants,

William Wagner,
James S. Granger,

Christian Herlocker,
Oliver E. Peters.

Corporals,

Alexander Doran,
Edmund Dague,
Samuel Doran,

George Daily,
John N. Miller,
Lucius C. Smith,

George B. Sisco.

Musicians,

William K. Evans

James M. Strasburg,

Wagoner,
Joseph Coil.

Privates,

Adair, Joseph M.
Absent, sick, since May 7, 1864.
Bear, Lemuel.
Bear, Jacob.
Beecher, John J.
Berger, Samuel R.
Blanvelt, Henry.
Brown, Samuel.
Burwell, Walter.
Campher, Jacob.
Cook, Jacob.
Cook, George.
Cooly, David.
Crist, Vandemark.
Cring, Henry.
Dague, Levi.
Dague, Daniel.
Dague, Benjamin.
Dodd, Thomas C.
Drake, Frank.
Early, Martin.
Evans, Alvin B.
Absent, sick in hospital at Pittsburg, Pa.
Fisher, Joseph, Sr.
Frable, Quincy.
Friend, Frank.
Goodrich, Justus.
Gravina, Charles F.
Guerin, Lovett T.
Hartrem, Benjamin.
Hendrickson, Daniel.
Hogbin, John M.
Irwin, Samuel.
Jacobs, John W.
Johnson, Charles W.
Johnson, Thomas A.
Johnson, William H.
Jones, Abner F.
Died Aug. 13, 1864, on steamer United States, en route to Washington from Fort Powhatan, Va.
King, Levi.
Klick, Ephraim.
Landon, George W.
Landon, David.
Landon, Wellington C.
Landon, Hannibal.
Landon, John D.
Died Aug. 16, 1864, at Smithville, Ohio.
McCloud, Charles W.
McCurdy, Henry H.
Marion, George.
Meeks, Benjamin.
Miller, Reuben F.
Miller, James R.
Miller, George W.
Miller, Peter.
Miller, Philip.
Miller, John J.
Absent, sick in hospital at Washington, D. C.
Miller, Edward.
Moore, William S. G.
Ogden, Charles S.
O'Kane, Henry.
Osborne, Ezra L.
Patterson, Jerome.
Phelps, Alfred.
Priest, Silas.
Ranny, John H.
Rarice, Joseph.
Roberts, James.
Died Aug. 15, 1864, in hospital at Washington, D. C.
Sheldon, Bennett.
Somers, George.
Smith, Henry.
Smith, Isaac N.
Absent, sick in hospital at Washington, D. C.
Smith, John W.
Smith, Stephen G.
Smith, William.
Smith, Daniel O.
Smith, Aaron.
Smith, Joseph.
Strayer, Abraham.
Strasburg, James.
Ulry, George D.
Weatherby, Samuel S.
Wilkins, Nelson.
Wilson, William S.
Absent, sick in hospital at Washington, D.C.

COMPANY C.

Captain,
Lawrence L. Meachem.

First Lieutenant,
Henry A. Guitner.

Second Lieutenant,
Sawyer A. Hutchinson.

First Sergeant,
William J. Gill.

Sergeants,

Charles H. Kirk,
Theodore Tibbetts,

Menzes P. Gillespie,
Charles W. Smith.
Died Aug. 4, 1864, at Fortress Monroe, Va.

Corporals,

Chauncey W. Phelps,
William O. Guitner,
George W. Robison,
James A. Ranney,

Irvin A. Lawson,
John B. Cornell,
Albert Mattoon,
Newell W. Grinnell.

Musicians,

David A. Schaff,

Calvin P. Weaver.

Wagoner,
Andrew Adams,

Privates,

Allen, Thomas J.
Alexander, James.
Ambrose, Henry.
Bartels, William Y.
Bartels, Peter B.
Died Aug. 12, 1864, at Fortress Monroe, Va.
Brinkerhoff, Uriah.
Brinkerhoff, Stephen.
Bryant, Charles W.
Carver, Joseph.
Clarke, Edwin E.
Clark, James R.
Absent, sick in hospital at Washington, D.C.
Clark, William.
Clarke, George W.
Discharged May 7, 1864, on Surgeon's certificate of disability.
Clapham, William.
Clapham, Milton.
Crout, Lewis B.
Davis, Edwin F.
Drake, Frank.
Discharged May 7, 1864, on Surgeon's certificate of disability.
Dusenbury, Daniel.
Dyxon, Irvin W.
Dyxon, Clinton.
Ferris, Joseph E.
Foutz, John N.
Galley, James.
Getzendanner, James.
Gill, James.
Goldsmith, John.
Died July 18, 1864, at Bermuda Hundred, Va.
Gravinna, Fred. E.
Hagar, Luther P.
Hawkins, Withing.

Holmes, John.
Hutches, Jasper N.
Died July 20, 1864, at Bermuda Hundred, Va.
Kiner, Francis M.
Kritzinger, George W.
Landon, William.
Miller, William.
Promoted to Hospital Steward June 25, 1864.
Noble, John.
Oldham, Austin W.
Perry, George.
Pinney, Horace D.
Pinney, Grove W.
Pinney, John H.
Died July 15, 1864, at Fort Powhatan, Va.
Ranney, David.
Ranney, Joel.
Riley, Lucius R.
Rose, Seth C.
Schrock, Homer.
Schrock, Vause.
Schrock, Joseph.
Scoby, Gideon.
Smith, Daniel.
Spring, Homer.
Strong, Stephen.
Toby, William O.
Absent, sick in hospital at Washington, D.C.
Vance, Edward P.
Waters, John B.
Died Aug. 10, 1864, at Fortress Monroe, Va.
Watson, Warren W.
Washburn, Riley.
Wright, Samuel.

COMPANY D.

Captain,
Hiram C. Tipton.

First Lieutenant,
Henry L. Whitehead.

Second Lieutenant,
John M. Dickerson.

First Sergeant,
Nathan D. Mitchell.

Sergeants,

John Q. Landes,
James P. Hay,

Jasper R. Manning,
Thomas T Ferguson.

Corporals,

John Spangler,
John Chaffin,
Armenas F. Kilbury,
Adin H. Walton,

Richard VanHorn,
Thomas Chenoweth,
George W. Davis,
Benjamin Sands.

Privates,

Adams, John Q.
Atchison, Charles P.
Baird, Simon S.
Ballard, Thomas H.
Basket, David.
Bertsch, John.
Bozenrife, James.
Brown, John.
Bullen, William.
Clark, David.
Cline, Emanuel.
Coffman, Quintillius P.
Dalby, Isaac N.
Deyo, Amos.
Died Aug. 13, 1864, at Baltimore, Md.
Dickerson, Thomas C.
Edginton, Joseph.
Engler, Joseph.
Fellows, Theodore B.
Fleming, Llewellyn.
Freeman, Richard P.
Freeman, Charles H.
Freese, Andrew J.
Gardner, George
Gardner, James P
Gilliland, Hamilton.
Gilliland, Harrison.
Absent, sick in hospital at Washington, D.C. No further record found.
Gilliland, John.
Died Aug. 7, 1864, at Fortress Monroe, Va.
Grisley, Charles.
Hann, Solomon.
Harper, Edward.
Howell, Jesse.
Huffman, John.
Ivy, James.
Kegg, John.
Keintz, Christian.
Kile, John.
Knaza, John.
Knida, William.
Kreitzer, Frederick.
Kroppf, Adolph.
Landes, Samuel.
Leighter, Zackey T.
Absent, sick in hospital at Washington, D. C.
Leightle, Josiah.
Lyda, Curtis.
McVaugh, Benjamin.
Miller, Isaac.
Montz, John.
Morton, Thomas.
Moses, Ebenezer.
Myers, Henry A.
Nutter, Loyd.
O'Day, Philip.
Poulson, William.
Price, Joseph.
Pugh, Richard.
Sells, Wilson S.
Schreves, James.
Southard, Thomas.
Souver, Isaiah.
Spangler, William.
Spangler, Calvin.
Spangler, Abraham.
Spangler, Alexander.
Timmons, Madison.
Timmons, Ira.
Thomson, Daniel.
Tracy, John N.
Waldo, George W.
Wampler, John.
Welfle, Augustus.
Wilkins, James.

COMPANY E.

Captain,
Ellis H. Heagler,

First Lieutenant,　　　　　　　　　　Second Lieutenant,
Jacob Romich.　　　　　　　　　　　　George W. Lakin.

First Sergeant,
John E. Price.

Sergeants,

James W. Michael,　　　　　　　　°Edward S. Churchman,
Samuel W. Lakin,　　　　　　　　　Charles Dantel.
　°Absent, sick at home. No further record found.

Corporals,

William Woods, Jr.　　　　　　　　John H. Snouffer,
Edwin R. Delashmutt,　　　　　　Robert A. Brelsford,
Lucas B. Goff,　　　　　　　　　　°William E. Gray,
Addison Adams,　　　　　　　　　Joseph H. Fisher.
　°Died May 12, 1864, of accidental gunshot wounds.

Musicians,

John Q. A. Brown,　　　　　　　　David Snouffer.

Wagoner,
William S. Adams.

Privates.

Andrus, Miner G.
Absent, sick in hospital at Washington, D.C. No further record found.
Ashbaugh, Hugh H.
Barker, David F.
Bannon, James
Bennett, Sheldon
Berry, Israel
Billingsley, William C.
Billingsley, William H.
Bowers, Newman H.
Brelsford, David H.
Brelsford, George W.
Bridges, Emery
Never mustered.
Bristol, Calvin E.
Bristol, George
Butterfield, Sylvester
Campnell, John
Case, Marcus
Cramer, John
Daniels, Morris
Died Aug. 16, 1864, in hospital at Washington, D.C., also borne on rolls as Moses Daniels.
Davis, Asa
Eldrick, David
Elliott, Jackson
Engle, William
Fuller, Reuben H.
Absent, sick at home; forwarded to regiment July 29, 1864, from Hampton Hospital. No further record found.
Gilbert, Henry
Groft, Michael
Grimes, Abraham A.
Hall, Nelson H.
Hodson, Henry
Johnson, Haslem F.
Absent, sick at home. No further record found.
Joslin, John
Lakin, Daniel C.
Lane, Benjamin F.
Lane, John D.
McCammel, William
Mateer, Washington
Absent, sick at home. No further record found.
Mateer, Samuel
Mateer, Robert G.
Mitchell, Charles
Needles, Henry
Payne, Edward
Pence, David M.
Pingree, Parker P.
Presley, Charles
Richards, Mathias H.
Snouffer, George B.
Snouffer, John B.
Somers, George
Stagg, Abraham
Sullivan, Samuel M.
Swayne, Emmit A.
Absent, sick at home. No further record found.
Thomas, Talton J.
Tuller, John T.
Vanderwert, Henry
Walcutt, Robert
Walcutt, William
Walters, Peter
Warner, John B.
Warner, George M.
Warner, George W.
Warner, John A.
Wilcox, John
Wilcox, Washington W.
Wilcox, Lawrence
Wilson, Joseph
Wilson, William E.
Wing, Frederick F.
Wiswell, John L. B.
Youel, Nathan C.

COMPANY F.

Captain,
Lewis H. Webster.

First Lieutenant,
Alonson N. Bull,

Second Lieutenant,
William S. Ridenhour

First Sergeant,
Wallace H. Moore

Sergeants,

Henry Zinn,
Franklin Spangler,

John Dugan,
Alexander Ross.

Corporals,

George Rader,
Richard M. Peckham,
George R. Furney,
Daniel Stelzer,

Francis S. Brady,
William Louis,
William Burwell,
Samuel Francis.

Musicians,

James M. Hauff,

Lucius Harris.

Wagoner,
Thomas Neiswinder.

Privates,

Allen, Marion
Arnold, Adam
Ault, James W.
Barkelew, Stephen
Bell, Robert
Clark, James
Coe, Levi
Coe, Daniel
Creighton, Wilson
Danforth, James
Dean, Frances B.
Dill, John
Dill, William.
Drake, Douglas
Drake, Charles
Field, Presley
Fishpaw, John L.
Foregrave, Robert G.
Fritter, Thomas
Garner, Clay
Gill, Frank
Gilland, —
Gregg, Joseph O.
Guither, Charles
Haden, Frederick A.
Haden, Frederick
Harris, Edwin
Harts, Jonas
Harper, Edward
Hays, Martin
Hays, Solomon
Hays, Samuel
Holt, Charles
Ingham, Orison
Innis, Jacob
Innis, William
Innis, Adam R.
Johnson, Theodore P.
Jones, Thomas F.
Keeler, James
Kirkpatrick, John
Krum, Philip
Krum, Harmon
Krum, Joseph
Landon, Chauncey P.
Laird, James
Absent, sick at Washington, D. C., since Aug. 14, 1864.
Lake, Norman
Leach, Asa
Leckrone, John
Lemon, Isaac
Neiswender, Henry
Nicholson, Horace
Nicholson, Merenus A.
Nickson, John
Park, Eugene
Patterson, Alonzo
Postle, Zaddock F.
Preston, Willard
Price, Oliver P.
Raber, John
Rees, Joseph H.
Rees, Egbert
Ridenour, John
Died Aug. 12, 1864, at Fortress Monroe, Va.
Ridenhour, David
Ross, William H.
Shafer, Lyman
Shiffler, George
Shrum, Russell
Shull, Solomon
Died Aug. 4, 1864, at Fortress Monroe, Va.
Smith, John W.
Staadt, John
Starrett, Nathaniel
Stelzer, John
Stelzer, Adam
Stygler, Leander G.
Suver, Isaac
Walker, Joseph
Washaw, Theodore
Washburn, Riley W.
Webber, Frederick
Wengert, John
Westervelt, Howard
Whip, George, Jr.
Wilcox, Lucius
Wilson, William
Wolbert, George
Zane, Corbin

COMPANY G.

Captain,
Edward W. Fisher,

First Lieutenant,
Robert S. Boyles.

Second Lieutenant,
William H. Zarbaugh.

First Sergeant,
Sylvester M. Sherman.

Sergeants,

David Culp,
John Boyles,

John McConnell,
Dimmick Harris.

Corporals,

Russell B. Heller,
Garnett Whitelock,
Henry C. Bennett,
*Peter Redfern,
*Absent, sick at Washington, D. C.

John Morehead,
John H. King,
Joseph Shaaf,
Robert Edwards.

Musician,
Urias Jones,

Wagoner,
Theodore Wareham,

Privates,

Alban, John M.
Anderson, Hiram
Augst, John S.
Bachtel, John
Bare, Daniel
Bare, Jones M.
Barley, George
Brown, Franklin
Bryan, Daniel
Bushong, William
Bushong, Isaac
Bultz, Daniel
Cheesman, Welcome
Clark, Charles
Absent, sick in hospital at Washington, D. C.
Clemens, James C.
Cloud, Robert W.
Cook, George J.
Cooper, Isaac
Cooper, Jacob
Coover, Wilson G.
Absent, sick in hospital at Washington, D. C.
Cromwell, Richard T.
Davidson, Alfred
Dillinger, Abraham
Absent, sick in hospital at Washington, D. C.
Downs, Henry
Dutcher, William J.
Edwards, Daniel
Ensminger, Allen A.
Foreman, Daniel
Foreman, Joseph J.
Haines, David
Hart, John
Harbaugh, Joseph
Harkness, Garrett
Harper, Edward
Hickman, Joseph S.
Jones, Zedekiah
Kempher, John
Kesse, Jacob
Lake, Elijah
Lake, Jesse
Lintner, Casper
Lover, George W.
McKinsie, William
Marcle, Elijah C.
Meyers, Arnold
Miller, John
Miller, William
Moore, John W.
Moorehead, John
Moorehead, William S.
Moorehead, Philip C.
Mosier, Samuel
Overholt, David F.
Perry, Aristus
Petty, Franklin
Poe, Ebenezer W.
Rogers, Elijah F.
Shelley, Daniel
Snare, Joseph
Spangler, Benival
Spangler, Martin
Died Aug. 14, 1864, at Fortress Monroe, Va.
Stambaugh, Richard
Steen, James
Stoner, Martin O.
Taylor, John W.
Taylor, John
Taylor, Robert
Absent, sick in hospital at Washington, D. C.
Travis, Calvin
Van Sicle, Isaac
Warner, Daniel
Whight, Eli
Willick, John
Williams, Samuel J.
Wilson, David M.
Wineland, George W.
Died August 13, 1864, on board steamer at Alexandria, Va.

— 161 —

COMPANY H.

Captain,
Samuel W. Williams,

First Lieutenant,　　　　　　　　　　　Second Lieutenant,
Charles H. Parsons.　　　　　　　　　　William H. Miller.

First Sergeant,
Charles H. Decker,

Sergeants,

Leo. Lesquereux, Jr.,　　　　　　　　　Orestes A. B. Senter,
Alfred Rietson,　　　　　　　　　　　　Robert E. Sheldon.

Corporals,

Charles Butler,　　　　　　　　　　　　Richard H. Levitt,
Samuel A. Decker,　　　　　　　　　　Henry O'Kane,
James Glover,　　　　　　　　　　　　Addison G. McKee,
Mannassa Jones,　　　　　　　　　　　John S. Roberts.

Musicians,

Robert Dawson,　　　　　　　　　　　　James M. Goss.

Wagoner,
Oris B. Galloway.

Privates,

Allen, Silas
Allison, George
Andrews, William H.
Aspinwall, Sterne F.
Avons, Charles F.
Barnhart, Charles
Bennigmese, George
Bergin, Charles S.
Booth, Howard L.
Booth, Morris
Bright, George W.
Brown, Rufus
Byown, Alexander
Brownson, Orrin S.
Bruck, Philip
Butler, Nathan
Davis, Charles
Dawson, William
Douglass, Jerry
Emrich, Henry
Fence, William
Fickel, Robert
Frass, Henry
Harrison, Joseph
Helsel, John
Hennessey, Samuel
Hill, Henry
Howard, William H.
Hubbard, John H.
Humphries, Benjamin F.
Hume, Wilson
Hurd, Edward
Innis, Henry M.
Jones, William S.
Lewis, William
McKenzie, William
Minor, Edward
Morton, Robert H.
Morrison, Robert
Murray, Theodore
Neville, Morgan
Oldham, James
Pace, John M.
Parks, Samuel
Parsons, Frank R.
Peters, Samuel
Pierce, Stephen
Pickering, Amos J.
Powell, John E.
Rapp, Gregory
Ridgway, William S.
Seibert, Charles
Scott, Henry
Shewry, Charles W.
Stickney, Henry
Thomas, Claudius
Trunnel, Albert
Tuller, John T.
Volk, John H.
Westwater, Robert M.
White, George
Williams, Elijah J.
Wing, Henry W.
Wolcott, Horace W.
Wooley, William P.
Wooley, John

COMPANY I.

Captains,
Henry Plimpton.   Benjamin C. Stratton.   James A. Stockton.

First Sergeant,
Lucien G. Thrall.

Sergeants,
°Perry Hodgden,   °William H. Paul,
Joseph T. Hays,   William H. Underwood.
°Absent, sick in hospital at Washington, D. C.

Corporals,
David Deshler,   Charles H. Hathaway,
Abraham J. Evans,   Alonzo M. Morris,
Albert J. Frankenberg,   George Renick,
John T. Geary,   Benjamin VanHouten.

Musicians,
Henry W. Field,   Samuel Brittingham,

Wagoner,
Thomas W. Bryan,

Privates,

Albright, Jacob
Anther, Thomas
Avery, Sylvester
Died Aug. 12, 1864, at Fortress Monroe, Va.
Bailey, Thomas
Bancroft, George D.
Beekey, William
Died Aug. 13, 1864, at Washington, D. C.
Bierley, Andrew
Bortle, Adam
Brown, Elbert C.
Brown, William D.
Brown, John
Coleman, George W.
Davidson, John S.
Wounded June 16, 1864, at Waugh's Church, near Point of Rocks.
Dickson, Adelbert
Dunbar, Charles B.
Dunn, John
Eicholds, Zachariah
Ender, John
Erlenbush, Herman
Fell, John
Fisher, Siron
Grate, Gustavus S.
Groff, Thomas F.
Hirshey, John M.
Hikes, John
Absent, sick in hospital at Washington, D. C.
Howle, Charles A.
Hymrod, Albert
Jones, Henry E.
Kinnell, Adam
King, John A.
Lawson, Jacob
Lewis, William G.
Lisk, Cornelius
Absent, sick at home.
Looker, Jonathan
Lytle, Nathaniel
Mayes, Charles L.
Mallory, Ogden
Absent, sick in hospital at Pittsburgh, Pa.
Messerly, Silas
Moccobee, Gazaway
Moll, John R.
Moore, George F.
Montgomery, Edward
Absent, sick in hospital at Washington, D. C.
Morse, Daniel L.
Morris, Amos V.
Noe, Andrew J.
Neereamer, Otis
Otstot, Daniel
Preston, Milligan A.
Absent, sick.
Renner, Andrew
Ricketts, Charles F.
Roberts, Griffin
Rohrer, Samuel B.
Sager, John
Sells, Basil
Sells, Joseph M.
Seibert, Lewis
Smith, Howard C.
Snyder, Francis T.
Spade, Samuel
Stephens, James
Stewart, Edward K.
Tufts, Cyrus
Absent, sick.
Watt, Henry
Whitacre, John E.
Died July 28, 1864, in hospital at Fortress Monroe, Va.
Williams, Henry
Williamson, James W.
Williard, Charles D.

COMPANY K.

Captain,

Thomas Lilley.

Died July 24, 1864, at Bermuda Hundred, Va.

First Lieutenant.
David Roberts.

Second Lieutenant,
John H. Fearn,

First Sergeant,

Orrin Mansfield.

Sergeants,

John W. Swisher,
Adam M. Rarey,

Ralph Hamner,
John Cox.

Corporals.

William S. Hopkins,
Henry Easterday.
William H. Kile,
Thomas Begg,

John P. Sharp,
Andrew J. Smith,
Thomas J. Harwood,
Charles W. Fairrington.

Musicians,

William C. Gill,

Edward Hoffman.

Wagoner,

James Sandy.

Privates,

Behm, Edward G.
Bradfield, Morris
Byrns, James
Burnham, Robert
Campbell, Charles
Chandler, William
Conrad, Solomon
Coplin, Obediah
Cramer, William
Cummins, Edward
Cummins, John
Davis, George
Davidson, James R.
Davidson, Constantine
Dildine, George H.
Donaldson, Judea W. D.
Egleburger, Albert
Ellis, Jeremiah
Evans, Benjamin W.
Ferguson, Lawrence
Fisher, William
Foreman, Edward R.
Forsythe, William
Gardner, James W.
Gardner, Joseph C.
Goods, Robert W.
Goodson, William J.
Goff, Tillman
Hedrick, Levi
Henderson, Abner
Hitler, Eli
Jackson, Aaron
Kalb, Albert
Kile, Robert A.
Kile, James A.

King, John
Kraner, Andrew D.
Latimore, Thomas
Lilley, Philip
Lilley, James
Loos, John C.
Lukens, Alfred
Lukens, Harrison
McClish, Henry
Mansfield, George
Mason, Solomon
Morehead, Louis
Noftzger, Christ
Oldham, Samuel
Oldham, James
Pendleton, James G.
Roan, John
Schranger, John W.
Scott, John W.
Sharp, John G. Absent, sick at home.
Shockley, William Absent, sick at home.
South, Samuel
Swisher, Erwin T.
Toy, Nathan P.
Townsend, Milby
Townsend, William
Vance, Nathan
White, William
Whitsel, Henry
Willie, Robert L.
Winehart, Hiram
Wycuff, William
Yarger, Jacob

ROLL OF HONOR

133RD REGIMENT OHIO VOLUNTEER INFANTRY.

Names.	Co.	Rank.	Died.	Buried.	Remarks.
Avery, Sylvester.	I	Private.	Aug. 12, '64	Hampton, Va.	Died at Fortress Monroe, Va. Interred in sect'n —, row —, grave 44.
Bartels, Peter B.	C	Private.	Aug. 12, '64	Hampton, Va.	Died at Fortress Monroe, Va. Interred in sect'n D, row 23, grave 13.
Beekey, William.	I	Private.	Aug. 13, '64	Arlington, Va	Died at Washington, D.C.
Clark, Joseph M.	..	Major.	Aug. 31, '64	Columbus, O.	Died at Fortress Monroe, Interred at Greenlawn Cemetery
Daniels, Morris M.	E	Private.	Aug. 16, '64	Arlington, Va	Died at Washington, D.C.
Deyo, Amos.	D	Private.	Aug. 13, '64	Baltimore, Md	Interred in Louden Park Cemetery.
Drake, John W.	A	Private.	July 4, '64	. . . .	Died at New Creek, W. Va.
Drake, William.	A	Private.	June 8, '64	. . . .	Died at New Creek, W. Va.
Garner, William.	A	Private.	Aug. 7, '64	. . . .	
Gilliland, John.	D	Private.	Aug. 7, '64	Hampton, Va.	Died at Fortress Monroe, Va. Interred in sec'n D, row 24, grave 21.
Goldsmith, John.	C	Private.	July 18, '64	Petersb'rg, Va	Died at Bermuda Hundred, Va. Interred in Poplar Grove Cem'try.
Gray, William E.	E	Corporal	May 12, '64	. . . .	Died of ac'dent'l wo'nds.
Harris, Samuel.	A	Private.	June 16, '64	. . . .	Died at New Creek, W. Va.
Hutches, Jasper N.	C	Private.	July 20, '64	Petersb'rg, Va	Died at Bermuda Hundred, Va. Interred in Poplar Grove Cem'try.
Jones, Abner F.	B	Private.	Aug. 13, '64	. . . .	Died on steamer United States.
Landon, John D.	B	Private.	Aug. 16, '64	. . . .	Died at Smithv'le, Fr'klin County, O.
Lilley, Thomas.	K	Captain	July 24, '64	Petersb'rg, Va	Died at Bermuda Hundred, Va. Interred in Poplar Grove Cem'try.
Pinney, John H.	C	Private.	July 15, '64	. . . .	Died at Fort Powhatan, Va.
Ransbottom H'nry	A	Private.	July 30, '64	Hampton, Va.	Died at Fortress Monroe, Va. Interred in sec'n D, row 22, grave 10.
Ridenour, John.	F	Private.	Aug. 12, '64	Hampton, Va.	Died at Fortress Monroe, Va.
Roberts, James.	B	Private.	Aug. 15, '64	Arlington, Va	Died at Washington, D.C.
Shull, Solomon.	F	Private.	Aug. 4, '64	Hampton, Va.	Died at Fortress Monroe, Va. Interred in sec'n E, row 14, grave 51.
Smith, Charles W.	C	Sergeant	Aug. 4, '64	Hampton, Va.	Died at Fortress Monroe, Va. Interred in sec'n E, row 15, grave 53.
Spangler, Martin.	G	Private.	Aug. 14, '64	Hampton, Va.	Died at Fortress Monroe, Va.
Waters, John B.	C	Private.	Aug. 10, '64	Hampton, Va.	Died at Fortress Monroe, Va. Interred in sec'n E, row 13, grave 41.
Whitacre, John E.	I	Private.	July 28, '64	Hampton, Va.	Died at Fortress Monroe, Va.
Wineland, Geo. W.	G	Private.	Aug. 13, '64	Arlington, Va	Died at Alexandria, Va.

www.ingramcontent.com/pod-product-compliance
Lightning Source LLC
Chambersburg PA
CBHW030244170426
43202CB00009B/616